Perspectives on Diversity, Equity, and Social Justice in Educational Leadership

ABOUT THE NATIONAL ASSOCIATION FOR MULTICULTURAL EDUCATION (NAME) SERIES

Editors: Abul Pitre and Ashraf Esmail

Educators in the twenty-first century face enormous challenges as a result of *No Child Left Behind* and *Race to the Top*. The requirements embedded into these high account-ability policies have exacerbated the disparities that exist in schools that serve histori-cally underserved students, particularly students of color. Educators are being tasked with raising test scores, and high-stakes testing along with prepackaged curriculum are placing educators and students in a psychic prison.

In this compelling series, we invite scholars and practitioners to address issues of diversity, equity, and social justice. The series seeks to provide books that will help educators to navigate the terrain of high-stakes testing that has resulted in the pedagogy of poverty. Drawing from critical multicultural education, the series invites scholars and practitioners who have an interest in critical pedagogy, critical race the-ory, antiracist education, religious diversity, critical theories in education, and social justice to provide practicing educators with knowledge to address the contemporary problems that have wreaked havoc on underserved students. This compelling series particularly speaks to practicing educators who hold positions as *leaders, teachers, counselors, coaches, mentors, paraprofessionals, and others involved with student learning.*

Perspectives on Diversity, Equity, and Social Justice in Educational Leadership

Edited by
Ashraf Esmail, Abul Pitre,
and
Antonette Aragon

ROWMAN & LITTLEFIELD
Lanham • Boulder • New York • London

Published by Rowman & Littlefield
A wholly owned subsidiary of The Rowman & Littlefield Publishing Group, Inc.
4501 Forbes Boulevard, Suite 200, Lanham, Maryland 20706
www.rowman.com

Unit A, Whitacre Mews, 26-34 Stannary Street, London SE11 4AB

British Library Cataloguing in Publication Information Available.

Library of Congress Cataloging-in-Publication Data Available

ISBN: 978-1-4758-3431-4 (cloth : alk. paper)
ISBN: 978-1-4758-3433-8 (pbk. : alk. paper)
ISBN: 978-1-4758-3434-5 (electronic)

♾™ The paper used in this publication meets the minimum requirements of American National Standard for Information Sciences—Permanence of Paper for Printed Library Materials, ANSI/NISO Z39.48-1992.

Printed in the United States of America.

Contents

Acknowledgments   vii

Introduction   ix
   Jasmine Williams

1 First, A Look Inside: Educational Leadership Student Perspectives
       on a Social Foundations Course   1
       Candace Thompson and Susan Catapono

2 Rocky Boats and Rainbows: Culturally Responsive Leadership
       from the Margin—An Autoethnography   23
       Ann E. Lopez

3 Change Your School, Change the World: The Role of School
       Leaders in Implementing Schoolwide Restorative Justice and
       Relational Pedagogies   43
       Martha Brown and Katherine Evans

4 White High School Administrators as Racial Advisors   63
       Bryan Davis

5 Changing Staff Attitudes through Leadership Development and
       Equity Teams   79
       Michelle Yvonne Szpara

6 Building Bridges or Isolating Families: When School Policies
       Conflict with Cultural Beliefs, Values, and Ways of Knowing 99
       María L. Gabriel

7 Principals, School Climate, and Social Justice: How State
   Compliance with National Initiatives May Not Be Enough   115
   Susan L. Dodd

8 Learning from Teachers: Critically Conscious Educational
   Leadership for Engaging Diverse Families in Title I Schools   127
   Cherrel Miller Dyce and Buffie Longmire-Avital

Index   149

About the Editors   153

About the Contributors   155

Acknowledgments

This inaugural book in the National Association for Multicultural Education (NAME) series has been a work in progress for several years. In 2012, a unique chapter in the history of NAME was forged when the series editors and Dr. Rose Duhon-Sells met with the Rowman and Littlefield team to finalize arrangements for the series. Under the visionary leadership of Dr. Rose Duhon-Sells, the NAME series became a reality paving the way for transformative scholarship that could improve the quality of education in the United States and abroad for diverse student populations. The editors for this inaugural volume are appreciative of the Rowman and Littlefield's Education (RLE) Team: Tom Koerner, Carlie Wall, Bethany Janka, and Sarah Jubar. A special thanks to Nancy Evans, a former member of the RLE team, who organized the initial meetings for the NAME series and to Sarah Jubar for making the series a reality with its inaugural book, *Perspectives on Diversity, Equity, and Social Justice in Educational Leadership*. Finally, we would like to thank all of the contributors for patiently revising and waiting for us to finalize the manuscript. You can now exhale—you have made history.

Introduction

Jasmine Williams

The student population in public schools over the past three decades has steadily grown more diverse racially, ethnically, and linguistically. According to the latest government statistics, minority students—a majority of whom come from lower socioeconomic families—now outnumber non-Hispanic white students (Banks, 2014). The diverse student population is in stark contrast to the homogeneity of teachers and administrators. They, conversely, are overwhelmingly white and middle class. Scholars contend that the racial and cultural dissonance between students, teachers, and administrators is largely attributable to disparate academic and social outcomes between white and minority students. The disparate outcomes, which far too often typify the minority experience in public schools, undergird the prominent positionality of social justice in educational leadership discourse.

Numerous schools of education, educator preparation programs, accreditation agencies, and education scholars have adopted social justice orientations. Hytten and Bettez (2011) point out that social justice is likewise included in educational reform proposals and job announcements. What does it mean for educational leadership to have the imprimatur of social justice?

Although there is no universal definition of social justice leadership, Kemp-Graham (2015) argues there are common themes. Most scholars would agree that social justice leaders adopt principles that place matters of inequity at the center of their advocacy (Kemp-Graham, 2015). Moreover, social justice leaders take conscious, deliberate actions to create school environments that confront and dismantle systemic inequalities, whether in campus and district policies or ingrained in school culture, and ensure that all students, particularly those that have been historically marginalized, are in educational surroundings that are equitable and inclusive. Social justice leadership is thus both philosophical and practical.

The emphasis on social justice leadership has great implications for educational practitioners at all levels, primary, secondary, and postsecondary. Yet despite its increasing prominence in educator preparation programs, there is evidence that challenges and concerns still exist in regard to its conceptualization and implementation by educational leaders (Hytten & Bettez, 2011; Katsarou, Picower, & Stovall, 2010; Kemp-Graham, 2015). In addition to the lack of a universal definition, there are two oft-repeated concerns.

The first is the application of social justice in abstract matters of vision and school philosophy and concrete matters of hiring practices and campus policies. The second is related to the concern of those who believe social justice is akin to an ideological litmus test; an extension of the social agenda of leftist radicals at colleges and universities or worse, hollow "feel good" words devoid of substance (Cochran-Smith, Barnatt, Lahann, Shakman, & Terrell, 2009; Heybach, 2009; Johnson & Johnson, 2007). Organized opposition to social justice in education was integral in its removal in 2006 from the nation's primary educator preparation accrediting agency's standards and dispositions (Heybach, 2009). Nonetheless, a plethora of researchers and scholars consider a social justice orientation necessitous if the goal is to truly create educational environments where all children thrive.

This brings us to this important and timely volume of scholarship for educational leaders. The discourses here, in their own way, address the aforementioned concerns regarding social justice in education. The emphasis is practical and experiential with realistic strategies and approaches for classroom teachers, campus and district administrators, leaders of educator preparation programs, and educational policy makers.

In chapter 1, Candace Thompson and Susan Catapano, professors at the University of North Carolina at Wilmington in North Carolina, argue that while much of the literature on social justice is concentrated on educator preparation programs and deservedly so, social justice also needs to be included in graduate programs that are preparing principals and superintendents. The chapter discusses a Social Foundations course at the doctoral level that critically examines past and contemporary school practices and policies and also critically examines the complex political nature of education. Thompson and Catapano insist principals and superintendents must embrace a social justice orientation in order for them to support classroom teachers.

In chapter 2, Ann E. Lopez, a native of Jamaica, is a faculty member at the University of Toronto in Canada. She uses the power of autoethnography to demonstrate how, in her role as a minority vice principal, she developed and applied critical consciousness in her experiences at Canadian schools with diverse student populations that had a monocultural teaching, support, and administrative staff. She discusses her approach to school policies that are incongruent to the goals of inclusion and social justice.

In chapter 3, Martha Brown, a doctoral student in Curriculum and Instruction from Florida Atlantic University, and Katherine Evans, faculty member at Eastern Mennonite University in Harrisonburg, Virginia, evaluate zero tolerance disciplinary practices that stereotypically are applied disparately to minority students. In their critique of these policies, they remind educators that students who are chronically disciplined cannot be effectively educated. Brown and Evans use the change theory paradigm to argue that the adoption of restorative justice and relational pedagogy will curtail suspensions and expulsions while positively impacting school operations and school culture.

In chapter 4, Bryan Davis, superintendent of the Columbus Wisconsin School District in Columbus, Wisconsin, uses a narrative approach to confront the challenges encountered by white school administrators in their role he defines as "racial advisors." Davis compellingly argues that all administrators, irrespective of their racial or ethnic background, function as racial advisors in their role as campus leaders, for example, through determining and enforcing policies related to student and staff behavior and discipline, and in the development of curriculum. Grounding his approach in transformational leadership theory, Davis identifies in practical terms, a framework within which white school administrators must position themselves in order for them to consciously and purposefully be successful in their role as racial advisors, and by extension, social justice educational leaders.

Staff development in social justice assumes center stage in chapter 5. Michelle Yvonne Szpara, in addition to her faculty responsibilities at Cabrini College in Radnor Pennsylvania, coordinates the Master of Education Program in Teaching and Learning. She highlights the roles of leadership and equity teams and how they can be embedded in professional development for monocultural staff that serves diverse student populations beyond race and ethnicity (i.e., differences in religion, philosophical beliefs, sexual orientation, and gender expressions). Szpara frames this work in transformational leadership as well.

Next in chapter 6, veteran educator María L. Gabriel who is coordinator of Equity and Diversity for the Poudre School District in Fort Collins, Colorado, uses a narrative approach to explore the relationship between schools and culturally and linguistically diverse families. She discusses the challenges school leaders encounter with the traditional model of family engagement and how those challenges ultimately inhibit the establishment of an equitable environment, thus hindering educational attainment for minority students. Gabriel then proposes a pathway for campus leaders to evaluate whether policies are "culturally responsive" in their creation, implementation, and communication to linguistically diverse families.

Susan L. Dodd a professor at St. Lawrence University in Potsdam, New York, in chapter 7 illustrates how state-mandated programs can be ineffectual in achieving social justice goals when they are constrained by limitation of resources. Instead, Dodd insists that educator preparation programs are the most appropriate vehicle for training school leaders in the creation of meaningful and sustained change. She also suggests potential avenues for partnerships between current school leaders and educator preparation programs.

Finally, in chapter 8, Cherrel Miller Dyce and Buffie Longmire-Avital, professors at Elon University in Elon, North Carolina, focus on school engagement with diverse families but from a different viewpoint. They offer study findings, from the perspective of teachers at a Title I school that suggest pragmatic measures principals and other educational leaders can adopt to improve the family engagement component of social justice. Dyce and Longmire-Avital's work is especially relevant given that Title I schools are required to develop engagement practices to comply with federal regulations.

There is consensus among scholars that more must be done to effectively serve the needs of all public school students. But as one of them writes, we cannot change that which we do not know. The value in this body of work is that social justice is considered from different experiences and dimensions for educational leaders. Moreover, the strategies and recommendations put forth are pragmatic and substantive. Continued discourse and scholarship that cast social justice in concrete terms increase the possibilities that students will be better served in our classrooms.

REFERENCES

Banks, J. A. (2014). *An introduction to multicultural education* (5th ed.). Boston, MA: Allyn and Bacon.

Cochran-Smith, M., Barnatt, J., Lahann, R., Shakman, K., & Terrell, D. (2009). Teacher education for social justice: Critiquing the critiques. In W. Ayers, T. Quinn, & D. Stovall (Eds.), *Handbook of social justice in education* (pp. 625–639). NY: Routledge.

Heybach, J. (2009). Rescuing social justice in education: A critique of the NCATE controversy. *Philosophical Studies in Education, 40*, 234–245.

Hytten, K., & Bettez, S. C. (2011). Understanding education for social justice. *Educational Foundations, 25*(1–2), 7–24.

Johnson, B., & Johnson, D. D. (2007). An analysis of NCATE's decision to drop "social justice." *Journal of Educational Controversy*, *2*(2), 1–9.

Katsarou, E., Picower, B., & Stovall, D. (2010). Acts of solidarity: Developing urban social justice educators in the struggle for quality public education. *Teacher Education Quarterly*, *37*(3), 137–153.

Kemp-Graham, K. Y. (2015). Missed opportunities: Preparing aspiring school leaders for bold social justice school leadership needed for 21st century schools. *International Journal of Educational Leadership Preparation*, *10*(21), 99–129.

Chapter One

First, A Look Inside

*Educational Leadership Student
Perspectives on a Social
Foundations Course*

Candace Thompson and
Susan Catapono

The paradox of education is precisely this—that as one begins to become conscious one begins to examine the society in which he is being educated. The purpose of education, finally, is to create in a person the ability to look at the world for himself, to make his own decisions, to say to himself this is black or this is white, to decide for himself whether there is a God in heaven or not. To ask questions of the universe, and then learn to live with those questions, is the way he achieves his own identity. But no society is really anxious to have that kind of person around.

—James Baldwin (1963), *A Talk to Teachers*, p. 42

INTRODUCTION

In a recent op-ed article on the commemoration of the Civil Rights Act, award-winning columnist, Leonard Pitts remarked on how the "complacent satisfaction" with progress that the nation has made in race relations and equality often overshadows the realities of the work still to be done. He states that those who praise the current state of racial equality, "mistake the way station for the destination" (2014, June 28)—dangerous stuff considering the systemic racism and discrimination that still permeates our legal, healthcare, political, and educational structures. Perhaps the "way station" metaphor can also be applied to current educational leadership preparation.

Amid a contentious political climate and calls for greater accountability and educational outcomes, the demand for educational leaders with ethical

1

fortitude, fiscal aptitude, and managerial and operational exactitude have become the way stations of what we celebrate as successful leadership. We have become complacent with this narrative and its vague language of celebratory diversity; complacent in our misplaced satisfaction with educational policy and leaders when reports of increasing test scores suggest that we are in fact ensuring that all children can learn. It is true that some progress in leadership preparation has been made using a social justice framework and centering issues of race, gender, and class, but this progress never quite reaches the path to a more equitable and socially just destination.

The expectation that school leaders, principals, district-level experts, and superintendents will set a tone for understanding and embracing diversity, equity, and social justice is expected but is rarely the reality. Despite the growing body of research on the need for and impact of leadership preparation, that weaves a transformative diversity and social justice framework throughout leadership programs (for example, Andrews & Grogan, 2001; Brown, 2004; Cambron-McCabe & McCarthy, 2005; Capper, Theoharis, & Sebastian, 2006; Dantley, 2002; Furman, 2012; Hawley & James, 2010; Jean-Marie, Normore, & Brooks, 2009; McKenzie et al., 2008; Pitre, 2014), many school leaders still do not understand or recognize the urgency of establishing school culture and communities that are conscious and inclusive of diverse cultures and lifestyles.

This may be attributed to a lack of information in their preparation or a calculated desire to maintain the status quo. Whatever the reason, school leaders are clearly under pressure to enact policies and curriculum that adhere to the latest political mandate (Jean-Marie et al., 2009). Their focus is on technical leadership and meeting state and federal mandates for accountability for student progress rather than the moral leadership and reform so desperately needed in schools so all learners are supported and successful (Theoharis, 2007).

We maintain that despite the pressures of policy and reform, leaders and those who prepare them do not have to become subservient to the process. Educational leaders must become conscious and skilled actors in subversive, and yes, even joyful leadership. Schools of education have a responsibility to prepare school leaders to lead not only in curriculum and administration but also in addressing systemic inequities and making a place for children and families from diverse cultures, family dynamics, and perspectives.

What is needed is a disruption of the usual operational responses to market-driven, high stakes accountability, and more of what Blackmore (2006) calls a transformative discourse of diversity that shifts the market-driven narrative to one focused on issues of social justice and a deep understanding—and, more importantly, action—that resists a narrowed vision of equity and conceptions of power and privilege. Moreover, there is a need to move beyond technical leadership that "tends to view the existing social order as legitimate" (Riehl, 2000, 58).

What is needed is a move beyond the self-satisfied way station to one with the disruptive uncertainty of borderlands where critical questions are posed and engaged, worldviews are challenged, and the usual is interrogated so that aspiring leaders may grapple with these issues causing them to "understand their ethical and moral obligations to create schools that promote and deliver social justice" (Andrews & Grogan, 2001, p. 24).

This chapter examines one attempt to disrupt the traditional preparation of educational leaders in a Doctorate in Educational Leadership (Ed.D.) Program at a southeastern public university that included a new course in social foundations as part of the required set of courses for all students (i.e., educational administration, curriculum and instruction, and higher education).

We—an instructor and codeveloper of the course and the chair of the Department of Educational Leadership—discuss students' perspectives on the social foundations course and their engagement in critical cultural analyses examining the ideological, cultural, sociopolitical, and economic contexts of schools and society using theoretical and field-based case studies, cross-cultural interviews, media analyses, and policy analyses. Study findings suggest that integrating educational foundations content that examines past and contemporary school practices, educational policy, and reflections on the relationship between policy, identity, and practice can help students develop strategies for moving from critical thought and dialogue to informed action.

SCHOOL LEADERSHIP FOR SOCIAL CHANGE

> I haven't considered this material (issues of social justice) since I was in my undergraduate teacher education program. Actually, we didn't really talk about it then. This topic (supporting students with different sexual orientation) isn't something we have ever talked about. This has really opened my eyes and informed me about I need to be doing in my school.
>
> —Current Ed.D. student and assistant principal, fall 2013

Doctoral programs like ours, with a focus on school administration, tend to attract a large number of school-based personnel who aspire to leadership roles. These teachers, assistant principals, and principals have spent time in classrooms and see their next career move as the central office. As the student quoted above mentioned, rarely is the topic of diversity or social justice covered in myriad educational leadership courses in budgeting, human resource management, and strategic planning.

Even rarer is the likelihood that students on the educational leadership track will or have taken social foundations courses that help them contextualize and critically examine complex political, economic, and sociocultural issues surrounding education. This is an untapped opportunity to either revisit the social foundations of education that students explored as undergraduates or challenge them with information at a higher level when they are forming their leadership knowledge and developing leadership theories.

SOCIAL FOUNDATIONS

Social and multicultural foundations courses have the potential to impact students' cultural and social awareness and increase their propensity to move from individual understandings of racism, sexism, classism, and sexual orientation to understanding structural inequality at macro levels and working toward equity and access (Hardee, Thompson, Jennings, Aragon, & Brantmeier, 2012). The interdisciplinary nature of social foundations allows instructors and students "to apply disciplinary knowledge from the humanities and social science to understand and interpret "the meanings of education and schooling in diverse cultural contexts" (Tutwiler et al., 2013, p. 112).

School leaders engaged in social foundations courses can meet the challenge of school leadership and reform when given opportunities to acquire "key sociocultural knowledge" (Liggett, 2011, p. 326) through foundations courses that challenge them to think, reflect, and act from critical and multicultural perspectives (Ryan, 2006), to work against narrowed conceptions of education and schooling and the policies and practices that marginalize some populations while privileging others (Tutwiler et al., 2013).

Social foundations understanding is predicated upon the development of three perspectives: normative, interpretive, and critical. Together, these perspectives engage students and scholars alike in reflecting upon personal value orientations and assumptions, applying theoretical concepts from the humanities and social sciences to examine, understand, and explain education within different contexts, and in questioning educational and social assumptions and arrangements through a democratic lens to "assess educational beliefs, policies, and practices in light of their origins, influences, and consequences" (Tutwiler et al., 2013, p. 112).

These three perspectives represent an engaged and citizen-based praxis—a dialogic web of theory, reflection, and action in which we learn to read the world (Freire, 2000) and take action to remake and transform ourselves—the intrapersonal—and understand "systemic social justice issues, reflecting on these issues, and taking action to address them" (Furman, 2012, p. 203)—the extra personal.

Drawing from Freire and Furman's conceptions of praxis, the foundations course we developed is situated within a social justice framework that centers critical reflection, dialogue, and social action as powerful strategies for understanding, resisting, and transforming oppressive social arrangements in classrooms, schools, and society (Sheurich & Young, 1997). A social justice framework informs the social foundations student and scholar by challenging leaders to "make issues of race, class, gender, disability, sexual orientation, and other historically and currently marginalizing conditions in the U.S. central to their advocacy, leadership practices and vision" (Theoharis, 2007, p. 223). A theory of transformational learning aligns with this framework and provides an important foundation for student engagement in the difficult work of leadership for social justice.

Transformational Learning. Students in graduate educational leadership programs come to the table with eagerness and motivation to provide new leadership in schools struggling to the meet state mandates for progress and success while supporting the needs of a diverse student body. The first step in learning how to support the needs of individual learners is through understanding the rich and unique cultural perspective learners bring to school with them each day. School leaders typically reflect the demographics of teachers: that of white, middle-income, English-speaking Americans who have little experience working with children of color who may speak English as their second language or come from communities that are economically and culturally different from these white educators. Children from diverse backgrounds are struggling to make sense of a system that does not support their culture or their language.

School leaders are in a unique position to make school a welcoming place for children and their families with a relevant curriculum to help them succeed in life. However, many of these future school leaders have limited experience in how to develop schools that support diverse learners. To truly change their thinking around diversity and leadership, they must engage in deep, meaningful experiences that induce transformational learning. This is the highest level of learning that leads to a true shift in thinking (Hodge, 2014; Merriam, 2004; Mezirow, 2000b). This shift in thinking is the next level of cognitive development that occurs in adulthood (Merriam, 2004). Drawing from Mezirow's (2000b) work on transformational learning, Merriam notes,

> In transformational learning, one's values, beliefs, and assumptions compose the lens through which personal experience is mediated and made sense of. When this meaning is found to be inadequate in accommodating some life experience, through transformational learning it can be replaced with a new perspective. (p. 61)

Transformational learning will not occur as a result of experiences only and must be combined with reflection and discourse (Feinstein, 2004; Merriam, 2004). Premise reflection (Mezirow, 1991) moves beyond merely thinking about what has happened to considering what has happened within a social context. Reflection at this level requires knowledge of and reflection on the current "socially constructed assumptions, beliefs, and values about the experience or problem" (Merriam, 2001).

Discourse comes next and the person engaged in critical reflection must discuss and evaluate what has happened, how it fits into both the socially constructed norms and the need for change—what should become the social norms. The flow and language of the discourse must be new, with those participating taking risks as they discuss subjects and ideas that are uncomfortable and in ways and with people who may or may not share their views (Kucukaydin & Cranton, 2013).

This new way of discussing and evaluating leads to new understanding and the student of educational leadership shifts his or her thinking from what is to what it should be and further, to what actions they can take to change it. An example of this process was described when one student in this study discussed her observation of students at her high school who cannot graduate without passing four, progressively difficult, mathematics courses. She said she started to ask why that was necessary if the student is not going on to a career that would require Calculus. She also discussed with the principal how many students—particularly students of color—were dropping out of school because they could not meet this requirement.

In a process of transformational learning, both reflection and discourse must have support through critical friends, knowledgeable guides, and mentors who both support and challenge the thinking. Resistance to new or different thinking is not considered a negative reaction; rather it is a "natural response to transformational learning pedagogy, which, if addressed, promotes learning" (Young, Mountford, & Skrla, 2006, p. 265). The student mentioned above hopes to study and suggest revisions to the mathematics curriculum and requirements as her dissertation. As an emerging leader for diversity, she wants to disrupt the dropout rate because of course requirements.

Leadership for Diversity. Yet, how to move new school leaders to this point of transformational learning, reflecting, and discussing ideas that are not part of the current social context? This is especially difficult when many school leadership programs are composed of a variety of courses that prepare school leaders to manage a school or a district rather than lead for reform and inclusion of all learners (Jean-Marie et al., 2009; McClellan & Dominguez, 2006). Courses in budget, finance, law, and organizational development are common in school administrator programs typically leading to licensure for K–12 principals and in doctorate in educational leadership programs typically designed for superintendents and school district office positions. Rarely, if ever, are school leadership programs focused on societal issues, encouraging students to challenge the status quo, change the climate of schools so they are welcoming for all children and families, or "ensure they are accountable for the equitable treatment of all students" (McClellan & Dominguez, 2006, p. 227).

Further, faculty in graduate school leadership programs may have little experience in social and multicultural foundations, with many having been prepared for their positions through a combination of experience as school and district leaders, and successful completion of both a school administrator's licensure program and doctorate in educational leadership that reflect the goals and outcomes of the program where they are currently teaching and as a result of their preparation programs the status quo continues.

To disrupt this pattern, McClellan and Dominguez (2006) call for school administration programs to teach students how to work within the system to reshape the organization to one that will support the needs of the diverse students who are in attendance and be a critical observer of how bias and privilege work both within the institution of school and within themselves as leaders. A social foundations approach that develops normative, interpretive, and critical perspectives is vital to engaging professional educators in practices of democratic education that reclaim educators as ethical and transformative agents "envisioning and acting on needed educational and social reforms for pursuing and implementing educational equity and excellence in a culturally diverse society" (Tutwiler et al., 2013, p. 115).

BREAKING GROUND

Faculty in the Educational Leadership Department at this regional university, located in the Southeastern United States, met over a period of one academic year (2011–2012) to revise the Doctorate in Educational Leadership. The revision added an additional concentration of Curriculum and Instruction to the single concentration of Educational Administration that had been offered since the degree was first developed in 2006. The first cohort in the Ed.D. started classes in fall of 2007, with sixteen students.

The program was unique in the requirement for students to complete three internships, including one with the business community and an international internship that had the students traveling to study education in Belize, London, or South Africa. The other courses in the program were typical of Ed.D. Programs, with goals that focused on school administration, such as budgeting, organizational development, and allocation of resources. The graduates were poised to serve as superintendents or school district office personnel. The addition of the Curriculum and Instruction concentration added a focus on curriculum development and opened the cohort to classroom teachers and content specialists, both at the PreK–12 school district and the community college.

The biggest change to the program, however, was not the new concentration, but the addition of a social foundation of education course at the doctoral level. A new dean hired in the college of education with a foundations background spurred the discussion in the department to include the course. Faculty focused on other programs in the department, at the master's level, advocated for a course in social justice. This was to the dismay of some faculty, especially those focused on school administration that resisted any course that they believed did not specifically prepare students for tasks they would encounter as a school leader. Topics in diversity, globalization, and culturally responsive teaching were considered "fluff" and not useful to a new administrator. After heated disagreements within the department, a social justice course was developed and added as an elective to all masters level programs; however, it was rarely offered due to other teaching demands of department faculty.

The Ed.D. program also established a core set of four classes of students in both concentrations would complete prior to moving into courses that focused on either educational administration or curriculum and instruction. The courses required included Social Foundations of Education, Leadership Theory, Organizational Development, and Applied Research. These four courses were offered in the first two semesters and served as induction courses for the program. Both students and educational leadership faculty responded to the social foundation course with mixed feelings. Some faculty raised comments about the course, questioned its purpose and why it was embedded in a doctorate in educational leadership.

Some faculty noted that the course belonged in an undergraduate program and took time away from the managerial courses offered at the doctorate level. One faculty became very upset and demanded the course be removed or offered as an elective because it was "a waste of time." This faculty member went so far as to discuss his views about the foundations course during his class on leadership theory. His class was offered on the same night and served as the companion class to social foundations. He attempted to convince students that the program was requiring a useless course and wasting their money.

Unfortunately, this impacted the perspectives of four students in the educational administration strand who enrolled in the fall 2012 foundations course. The students were resistant to the content and frequently displayed their discomfort and displeasure by not participating in class discussions or espousing opinions uniformed by the un-informed readings or research. Interestingly, though perhaps, not surprisingly, these four students are no longer enrolled in the doctoral program.

The new course for the doctorate program was designed and delivered by the social foundations faculty rather than educational leadership faculty—a rare occurrence in colleges of education given the marginalized role of foundations in teacher and leadership preparation programs and the propensity in leadership programs to circumvent foundations courses taught by foundations-educated faculty (deMarris & Tutwiler, 2013). This was a strategic move by the dean and chair to include other faculty in the delivery of the doctorate program and it allowed faculty in the Department of Educational Leadership to access expertise in the content without fanning the flames of discord within the department.

The course was designed in a hybrid format with students meeting on campus every other week and engaging in projects or informal virtual drop-in discussions during the weeks they were not on campus. The course combined rich interdisciplinary foundations theory with social justice and applied learning using case studies, fieldwork, individual research, media, and readings that included texts, research, and conceptual articles to challenge students' intrapersonal and extrapersonal assumptions, perspectives, positions, practices, and beliefs. Because none of the students in the two classes had prior knowledge of social foundations or what it involved, faculty included a description in the syllabus of what social foundations is, as well as engaged students in discussions about the role of foundations in developing normative, interpretative, and critical perspectives to guide student engagement with the material, each other, and their practice.

Over the course of the semester, students were required to read three main texts[1] as well as research articles and literature on historical and contemporary social justice issues centering race, ethnicity, language, class, gender, sexuality, and educational and social policy. Faculty believed this interdisciplinary breadth of material effectively captured a range of historical and contemporary perspectives to engage students from all leadership strands.

Course assignments were designed to illuminate and "talk back" to the readings and research and serve as opportunities for cognitive dissonance where, according to Shields, Larocque, and Oberg (as cited in Brown, 2004) students and faculty could "initiate conversations where problems and challenges may be identified and discussed" (2002, p. 130). The intent was to develop a course that offered opportunities for reflective analysis and dialogue with the critical examination of the historical roots of education and the enduring questions of fairness and equity in schooling and society that shape our present and inform how, who, and what we will lead to develop "action through policy praxis" (Brown, 2004, p. 96).

RESEARCH METHOD

In the spring of 2014, two faculty members studied the impact of the social foundation course on the first two cohorts of students' perspectives by using a qualitative approach that included individual interviews. The researchers specifically sought to gather information about the effect of the social foundation course on students and its possible role in helping to challenge, support, and develop culturally aware and responsive school leaders.

Class Demographics

Students from the fall 2012–2013 (n-21) and fall 2013–2014 (n-25) Social Foundations of Education course were invited to participate in a pilot study examining the impact of the course on their professional work, academic coursework, and perspectives. Of the forty-six students invited, fifteen (7 from fall 2012 and 8 from fall 2013) agreed to participate in a semi-structured interview to discuss their experiences in the course. Participants met with the researchers for approximately 45 minutes to 1 hour to share their views about the course, their perceptions of the effect the course had on their practice and approach to other courses in their programs, and if or how the course informed them as future school leaders attuned to social justice and diversity issues.

The interviews were recorded and researcher notes and interview transcripts were reviewed to identify emerging themes. Researchers first coded the data separately and then came together to compare and negotiate key themes that emerged from the data. The narrative results of the interviews revealed two main themes. These included (1) students' perceptions of diversity in relation to self and to community and environment and (2) students' perceptions of their ability to make a difference in their professional roles as a result of the course. Analysis of the two themes highlight the significance of the three education foundations perspectives—critical, normative, and interpretive in the preparation of educational leaders who recognize that education and life in a free society is a collective promise dependent upon citizens " … having the capacity to choose, the power to act to attain one's purposes, and the ability to help transform a world lived in common with others" (Greene, 1988, p. 32).

Author 1, who is also one of the course instructors, interviewed eight participants in this pilot study. These students were given the opportunity to speak with another researcher to avoid any implication of intimidation or discomfort, but each independently elected to be interviewed by the instructor and expressed confidence in their ability to be forthright in the interview. Table 1.1 provides an overview of participant demographics.

Table 1.1 Study Participant Demographics

Gender	Male	Female			
	1	14			
Ethnicity	White	Black	Latino		
	12	2	1		
Age Range	25–35	36–45	46–55	56–65	
	8	3	3	1	
Degree Concentration	Administration	Curriculum Instruction	Higher Education		
	0	8	7		
Employment	Elementary	Middle	Secondary	Postsecondary	Other
	6	0	2	6	1
Years of Experience	0–5 years	6–10 years	11–15 years	16–20 years	21+ years
	5	7	2	0	1

Study participants' worked in a diverse mix of educational environments. Four participants were teachers and instructional leaders in public PreK–5 elementary schools. Of those, two worked in schools serving a majority African American student population, one worked in a school with a balanced racial (50 percent AA/50 percent white) student profile, and one served a majority white student population.

Two participants worked in public high schools, both serving majority white student populations. Two participants worked in private or government schools with one teacher at a private parochial K–5 elementary school serving a majority white population and the other an Academically or Intellectually Gifted (AIG) coordinator at a Department of Defense PreK–5 school serving a racially and ethnically diverse population. The remaining seven participants worked in postsecondary settings. These included five at one predominantly white public university, one at a more diverse community college, and one at a nonprofit college preparation program.

Additional background information that the students provided beyond those listed in table 1 offered a contextual backdrop for understanding what knowledge and experiences the students brought to the course and how this might be enhanced by social foundations content. This included a description of the diversity of the student's work environment, reasons for choosing a career in education, qualities essential to professional success, experiences with diversity, and initial expectations of the foundations course.

Students' expectations of the course were tinged with apprehension. One African American participant stated, "I expected it to be where we talked about race, poverty and class and its impact on education in a majority white class. I expected it was going to be the same as before." This participant was referring to past experiences where she was often the only person of color in the room taking part in what she saw as superficial discussions about diversity. She continued, "… we talk about it [diversity], but it's really talking about it to get to the degree. Talking about the same thing, just going through the motions to complete the course requirements."

These expectations posed an initial challenge for foundations faculty in outlining and clarifying the goals, standards, and theoretical framework for understanding social foundations and its importance to educational leadership in examining "how issues of social justice (e.g., gender, race, ethnicity, sexual orientation, etc.) shape and influence possibilities and desires for a more harmonious society that transcends national and international boundaries" (Jean-Marie et al., 2009, p. 20). The themes discussed here illustrate how the social foundations pushes the boundaries of students' perceptions of self and understanding of diversity and social justice issues and shapes their capacity for agency in interrogating existing social arrangements and structures.

FINDINGS AND DISCUSSION

Two main themes emerged from the student interviews. The first theme, *Shades of Grey: Perceptions of Diversity* (Self) begins with an examination of students' perceptions of diversity within themselves; its subtheme, Perceptions of Diversity (Community and Professional Environments), is an examination of students' perceptions of diversity within their communities or professional environments.

In the second major theme, *We Make the Road by Walking: Perceptions of Ability to Make a Difference*, students discussed perceptions of their ability to make a difference in policy or practice, as a result of their participation in the foundations course. Within and across each theme, participants speak to the role that a praxis of critical reflection, dialogue, and action—using assignments as a problem-posing pedagogy—play in developing foundations perspectives and capacities for confronting issues of diversity and social justice in ways that interrogate "the democracy of decisions and administrative practices" (Dantley, 2008, p. 456).

Shades of Grey: Perceptions of Diversity

Standard in the National Policy Board for Educational Administration Standards for Advanced Programs in Educational Leadership for principals, superintendents, curriculum directors, and supervisors addresses the need for candidates to "work with all elements of the community." It emphasizes that "educational leaders must recognize, value, and communicate effectively with various cultural, ethnic, racial, and special interest groups" (p. 11). This requires knowledge of the various dimensions of diversity (i.e., race, ethnicity, class, gender, sexuality, ability, and language) and meaningful interactions and experiences with diverse populations.

Responses under this theme revealed how students grappled—through open and on-going dialogue—with self-perceptions of diversity knowledge and awareness regardless of previous experience with diversity. Many participants expressed surprise that their knowledge about diversity and social justice issues was not as extensive as they believed, with several commenting that they thought they knew a lot about diversity until they took the course. Phrases like "eye opening" and acknowledgment of "how little I really understood culture and diversity" were common. For example, an African American, female, former military, student in the age range of 56–65, said,

> You know, African American teachers—we tend to think we know everything about African Americanism. I had to step out of the box and take a new look, "I am African American, you can't tell me what it means to be African American." I had to step out. I also attended an all-Black college but there was a big gap between that time and this class—I just thought I knew it all, nobody can tell me the nature of me, I had to stop and tell self, "stop and listen to what people are saying."

Another example was particularly notable: Lara (a pseudonym), a white teacher at a predominantly black public elementary school whose first "real" experience with diversity began with the start of her teaching career. A significant turning point for Lara came in understanding the intersectionality of multiple dimensions of diversity and oppression and realizing how little she knew. She adds, "the [course] readings really made me challenge my own practice … made me wonder how many children have I not provided for? How much damage have I done not knowing and treating every student the same [color-blind approach]?" She says, "[w]hen I became a teacher is when I became aware of what diversity meant. Before that, it only meant race and religion."

Lara recalls as a younger woman, feeling like she "needed to stick with her own white, middle class people," but this changed with her first teaching job in a school with a large African American population. In her words, "I found myself loving my students … I became aware that every child is somebody else's child and deserved to be valued and understood." In taking the foundations course, Lara says, she "discovered that I didn't understand what diversity meant."

Prior experience with diversity in schooling, communities, and other activities may impact the level of familiarity with diversity that students had before taking the course. An African American participant working as an

assistant principal in a predominantly racially balanced school serving students from poor communities recalls growing up in a major Southeastern
city and feeling that there was a commitment to intentional diversity due
in part because of racial and economic quotas in North Carolina schools
at the time. She says, "There was a sense that there was a value in being
different—a recognition and appreciation of being different."

Unfortunately, this appreciation for and exposure to diversity is lacking in
her adult experiences. She says, "I was a NC teaching fellow [during under-
grad], and the only African American in a corps of 80 students!" Currently,
her school has two African American teachers and two African American
teaching assistants, "the only other blacks are either custodial or food service
staff. There are no other teachers or staff of color, so, diversity here is either
black or white."

Whether participants had extensive diversity-related experiences and
knowledge or were just beginning the process, the social foundations content
and course assignments (for example, the cross-cultural interviews, school-
curriculum survey, and critical media project) challenged the perspectives
of all study participants to engage in what Blackmore (2006) calls a transformative discourse of diversity, and in the words of one student, to "look
closely for who is included, how they are portrayed [in schools and curricu-
lum]." Confronting stereotypes and biases through reflection, dialogue, and
application—an important kind of action—is vital in leadership preparation
if students are to dismantle colorblind ideologies and make connections
between understanding diversity and moving toward a deeper examination
of equity and access (Brown, 2004; Diem & Carpenter, 2012; Niesche &
Keddie, 2011; Young et al., 2006).

Community and Professional Environments. Essential to a praxis centering dialogue of and about the dynamics difference is the continual process
of reflection. In this theme, students were asked to reflect on interactions with
and perspectives on diversity and issues of inclusiveness, equity, and access
in the communities and environments where they work. Students talked about
confronting assumptions about and awareness of diversity in groups and
individuals and grappling with their growing understandings of the interplay
between power and privilege. The responses under this theme reveal the
ways students used reflection to question personal assumptions and biases to
inform their professional practice and expand definitions of diversity from the
superficial to the complex. The following comment is illustrative of participants' thoughts on the role and impact of reflection embedded in the structure
of the course:

> The most impactful for me ... The reflective piece requiring that we reflect upon
> our own beliefs and values and experiences, and what we bring into schools and

into whatever position we're going to be in, and how that impacts what we're able to do for kids, and how we're perceived and how we think we're perceived.

Another student working in university admissions at a predominantly white university found the reflective requirements of the course challenging in "trying to relate course content to her [work] experience." She maintains that it was "challenging in a good way" as it "forced her to think critically and connect to her environment" and that it "took time to reflect upon and understand the impact [of content]."

Although most (twelve out of fifteen) of the students noted they had some understanding of diversity and social justice issues, many also said that diversity had been largely equated with race, class, and religion. Participants' limited view of diversity illuminates the need for understanding the intersectionality of oppression and a working knowledge of white privilege and the historical legacy of institutionalized inequality. As students reflect and analyze common inequities embedded in social and school policies and practices, such as the underrepresentation of students of color in advanced and honor classes or the overrepresentation of these same students in special education, they gain critical consciousness for action to interrupt and possibly transform unjust systems—demonstrating normative, interpretive, and critical stances.

For example, participants working in predominantly white PreK–12 schools noted that students of color are typically found in classes set aside for students not progressing on grade level. Ironically, these classes are called "on-level" classes. The Honor's or Advanced Placement classes are typically populated with white students. An African American elementary teacher noted:

> The students at my school are predominately White, middle-income students. This is represented in the AIG classes. In the EC classes [Exceptional Children-special education] there are more African American boys and girls. I know because there are so few African American children in my school and they are all in EC classes. Why? Surely there are AIG children who are Black?

Another participant, a teacher at a predominantly white public high school noted that sexual orientation is a struggle in local high school:

> Any difference is hard for high school students. No matter what it is—race, religion, sexual orientation, income level—it is hard for students to be different. There are some support groups, like a chapter of LBT, but the kids are still isolated if they identify with a "different" group.

Three white female participants working at a predominantly white public university reflected on what they noticed about their institution's lack of material commitment to diversity and inclusive learning environments. One

of the women, who works as an administrator in student health found it "…
troubling, when it's in [the university's] core values, statements, etc., but in
actuality there is little or no diversity. We say it's important, but our actions
don't necessarily support that." Participants' comments reflect frustration
as they come to recognize the disconnect between institutional rhetoric and
the disquieting injustices perpetuated in the wake of ineffective policies or
inaction, as revealed in this comment from an African American assistant
principal at a public elementary school:

> Racism is very embedded in this county… . I think people know about it, and
> I think and there's little being done about it. People are comfortable and compla-
> cent—black folks don't feel like fighting because they've been fighting forever.
> And they see that there really hasn't been much of a change. Everybody sees it,
> but nobody really knows what to do to combat it. I think there are small victories
> won and people trying to do things, but I don't anybody feels or sees that it's
> enough. … From the school board down there's still so much resistance, or how
> do we still end up with schools that are 99% poverty and 99% black in 2014?
> That's injustice! How does that even happen?

We Make the Road by Walking: Perceptions of Ability to Make a Difference

In the second theme, we explore participants' perceptions of their ability
to make a difference in their current roles and as future educational leaders. Using student perspectives on course assignments and the final project,
we found several examples where students discussed how the foundations
content impacted their practice and the ways they applied their knowledge
to interrupt hegemonic practices and policies. Course assignments were an
important element in instigating students' cognitive disequilibrium and facilitating their movement from critical reflection to critical action.

One student's comment that, "[I]t's important because people don't get
it. People have limited understanding of diversity and the intersectionality
of oppression," underscores the value of foundations content in shaping
students' thinking. Another participant who works with English Language
Learners (ELLs) at a community college added,

> The assignments [were the most impactful], especially the [cross-cultural]
> interview assignment—was a good experience in interviewing someone from
> another racial category and then transcribing, that, and reflecting on biases and
> assumptions about others.

A school-curriculum cultural audit assignment allowed students to examine the messages (explicit and inexplicit) included in various components of
school (PreK–12 and postsecondary) curricula (the formal and hidden) using

public spaces, print and web-based information, textbooks, and policy statements. This assignment was eye opening for postsecondary participants who elected to conduct the survey in a public school, and especially for PreK–12 participants who conducted the audit within their home schools. An example comes from one public elementary school administrator who conducted the survey in her school:

> It was way more difficult to do in my own school. I was like wow; I can't believe these challenges still exist, to what extent do I contribute to these, or cause more harm? Based on my experiences, should I be doing more? I think that reflection piece is always a challenge and thinking outside the box and from other people's perspectives and looking outside your own experiences.

Three examples of participants seeing a place to make a difference through their professional position included one student who is working with her high school administration to develop a ninth-grade academy to meet the needs of students who are struggling as they transition from eighth grade to high school. She noted that too many of the students of color in this group end up at the alternative high school in the district. She wants to keep them at the traditional high school with appropriate supports. This student noted:

> I come from a different culture [White, middle income]. I had to figure out how to teach young African American men. I had to re-think what I do and make my classroom a place where they can be successful.

Another example is a student who works at a community-based, nonprofit agency that supports K–12 students in their efforts to enter college. She works within a seven-region part of the state and works primarily with African America and Latino students in rural areas. Her area of focus, however, is on Native American students. This was the result of her work in the course's final project—a research paper and poster. Everything she has done since taking the course has focused on this group of marginalized students. She said,

> My employer started a pilot program working with [marginalized] students in three counties. I made sure they picked [county that serves a large number of Native American students]. The course and project made me more of an advocate for this group of students. One of the groups is not federally recognized so they cannot benefit from federal tribal resources.... . I thought I was interested in Latino students but found working with Native American students so interesting and necessary.

Finally, a third student, working at an elementary school with predominately white, middle-income students and families where she is the only African American teacher at the school, noted she has started speaking up and having honest conversations with the principal. Prior to taking the course, she said that she would ask questions but would not push back on the answers. Now, she is not content to accept the answers. She recalls one example:

> We have college day and we put the banners up from all the colleges. So I asked the person in charge, why no [Historically Black College or University], why no [local regional university without sports teams], why no community college? Maybe the students aren't going to go to top schools and more importantly, other students, especially those from low-income families or minority may not be able to go to one of those schools. Most kids start out now at the community college to save money. It was just wrong, such an example of ... [privilege?], yes, privilege. Before, I would have accepted the explanation that all kids can go to these colleges, this time, no, I said we have to do better and get all the opportunities displayed.

LEAVING THE WAY STATION: THOUGHTS ON MOVING FORWARD

Persistent inequalities in our educational system demand leaders with the capacity to think and to act critically. Leaders must be willing to continually reflect on their assumptions and perspectives and acquire the capacity to navigate the complex social, political, cultural, and environmental contexts in which schools are situated. The development and inclusion of a social foundations course in a doctorate in educational leadership program pushed students aspiring to lead their organizations to think about their own belief systems and the impact that their assumptions and biases can have on others who participate in the organization (Mezirow, 2000b).

Typically, courses in programs like this include how to manage the organization, focusing on tangible processes to develop the organization, manage the resources, and meet regulatory mandates. This course required students to consider new material for some and revisit material from their undergraduate programs for others. Yet, at this junction in their lives, they are preparing to be the one to lead in a setting that is comfortable with the status quo.

Within this structural-functionalist framework "that espouses the values of democracy and meritocracy, and that adopts a managerial orientation instead of a socially transformative one" (Riehl, 2000, p. 58), one who challenges these social arrangements is a necessary antidote. Using the tenants of social foundations to acquire normative, interpretive, and critical perspectives, educational leadership students engaged in uncomfortable class discussions, and realizing their own flawed thinking, began to look around and realize their participation in, and sometimes perpetuation of, cultural bias and marginalizing policies in themselves and their professional lives. This growing consciousness is an important foundation for informed action—the vehicle that propels us from the complacency of the way station.

Through a myriad of assigned readings and discourse, students interrogated their definitions of diversity, what it means to them personally, and what it means in their professional work. When connected to critical reflection and continuing dialogue, assignments and readings that engaged students in confronting injustice and institutional bias instigated important spaces for cognitive dissonance and critical consciousness. It is within these spaces that students began to determine what they could do to make a change—to disrupt the usual. Participants' comments illustrate the ways they began to interpret and critique: speaking up for the first time and asking difficult questions of themselves and the world. Some of the most transformative learning happened for people who thought they knew what it was like to be different but, as a result of this class, they were also confronted with their own biases and the complexity of diversity.

One course, out of many (twenty for this program) may or may not make a significant impact on future school leaders; however, the seeds are planted, and the research continues to see how the ideas and understandings that were started in the social foundations class flourish as these students continue through their program. We may, for the moment, take heart in the small awakenings witnessed in these young leaders, but we do not mistake this for the final destination. More research is needed on where these leaders may take this knowledge and what action they implement to make changes in their professional work that impact the lives of children and families. In 1963, James Baldwin wrote that, "the paradox of education is—that as one begins to become conscious one begins to examine the society in which he is being educated" (p. 42). In leaving the way station, we rise to meet this challenge in developing conscious leaders.

NOTE

1. Course texts included Jean Anyon's (2005) *Radical Possibilities: Public Policy, Urban Education, and a New Social Movement,* Lisa Delpit's (2012) *"Multiplication Is for White People": Raising Expectations for Other People's Children,* and Thomas King's (2005) *The Truth about Stories: Native Narratives.*

REFERENCES

Andrews, R., & Grogan, M. (2001). *Defining preparation and professional development for the future.* Paper commissioned for the first meeting of the National Commission for the Advancement of Educational Leadership Preparation, Racine, WI.

Baldwin, J. (1963). A talk to teachers. *The Saturday Review*, 39, 42–44. Retrieved from http://www.unz.org/Pub/SaturdayRev-1963dec21-00042?View=PDF.

Blackmore, J. 2006. Social justice and the study and practice of leadership in education. *Journal of Educational Administration and History*, 38(2), 185–200.

Brown, K. M. (2004). Leadership for social justice and equity: Weaving a transformative framework and pedagogy. *Educational Administration Quarterly*, 40, 79–110.

Cambron-McCabe, N., & McCarthy, M. M. (2005). Educating school leaders for social justice. *Educational Policy*, 19(1), 201–222. doi:10.1177/089590484271609

Capper, C. A., Theoharis, G., & Sebastian, J. (2006). Toward a framework for preparing leaders for social justice. *Journal of Educational Administration*, 44(3), 209–224.

Dantley, M. E. (2002). Uprooting and replacing positivism, the melting pot, multiculturalism, and other impotent notions in educational leadership through an African American perspective. *Education and Urban Society*, 34(3), 334–352.

Dantley, M. E. (2008). The 2007 Willower family lecture reconstructing leadership: Embracing a spiritual dimension. *Leadership and Policy in Schools*, 7(4), 451–460.

deMarris, K., & Tutwiler, S. W. (2013). Guest Editors' introduction. Critical, interpretive, and normative perspectives of educational foundations: Contributions for the 21st century. *Educational Studies*, 49, 104–106.

Diem, S., & Carpenter, B. W. (2012). Social Justice & Leadership Preparation: Developing a transformative curriculum. *Planning and Changing*, 43(1/2), 96–112.

Feinstein, B. C. (2004). Learning and transformation in the context of Hawaiian traditional ecological knowledge. *Adult Education Quarterly*, 54(2), 105–120.

Furman, G. (2012). Social justice leadership as praxis: Developing capacities through preparation programs. *Educational Administration Quarterly*, 48(2), 191–229. doi:10.1177/0013161X11427394

Freire, P. (2000). *Pedagogy of the oppressed* (M. B. Ramos, Trans., 30th ann. Ed). New York: Continuum.

Gay, G. (2007). The rhetoric and reality of NCLB. *Race Ethnicity and Education*, 10(3), 279–293. doi: 10.1080/13613320701503256

Greene, M. (1988). *The dialectic of freedom*. New York: Teachers College Press.

Hardee, S. C., Thompson, C. M., Jennings, L. B., Aragon, A., & Brantmeier, E. J. (2012). Teaching in the borderland: Critical practices in foundations courses. *Teaching Education*, 23(2), 215–234.

Hawley, W., & James, R. (2010). Diversity-responsive school leadership. *UCEA Review*, 52(3), 1–5.

Hodge, S. (2014). Transformative Learning as an "Inter-Practice" Phenomenon. *Adult Education Quarterly*, 64(2), 165–181.

Jean-Marie, G., Normore, A. H., & Brooks, J. S. (2009). Leadership for social justice: Preparing 21st century school leaders for a new social order. *Journal of Research on Leadership Education*, 4(1), 1–31.

Kucukaydin, I., & Cranton, P. (2013). Critically questioning the discourse of transformative learning theory. *Adult Education Quarterly*, 63(1), 43–56.

Liggett, T. (2011). Critical multicultural education and teacher sense of agency. *Teaching Education*, 22(2), 185–197.

Mezirow, J. (2000a). Learning to think like an adult: Core concepts of transformation theory. In J. Mezirow & Associates (Eds.), *Learning as transformation* (pp. 3–34). San Francisco, CA: Jossey-Bass.

Mezirow, J. (2000b). Learning as transformation: Critical perspectives on a theory in progress. San Francisco, CA: Jossey-Bass.

McClellan, R., & Dominguez, R. (2006). The uneven march toward social justice: Diversity, conflict, and complexity in educational administration programs. *Journal of Educational Administration*, 44(3), 225–238.

McKenzie, K., Christman, D., Hernandez, F., Fierro, E., Capper, C., Dantley, M., ... Scheurich, J. (2008). Educating leaders for social justice: A design for a comprehensive, social justice leadership preparation program. *Educational Administration Quarterly*, 44, 111–138.

Merriam, S. B. (2004). The role of cognitive development in Mezirow's transformational learning theory. *Adult Education Quarterly*, 55(1), 60–68.

Mezirow, J. (1991). *Transformative dimensions of adult learning*. San Francisco: Jossey-Bass.

Niesche, R., & Keddie, A. (2011). Foregrounding issues of equity and diversity in education. *Journal of Leadership & Management*, 31(1), 65–77.

Pitre, A. (2014). *Educational leaders in a multicultural society.* San Diego, CA: Congnella Academic Publishers.

Pitts, L. (2014, June 28). *Civil Rights journey far from over. Miami Herald.* Retrieved from http://www.miamiherald.com/2014/06/28/4206273/leonard-pitts-civil-rights-journey.html

Riehl, C. J. (2000). The principal's role in creating inclusive schools for diverse students: A review of normative, empirical, and critical literature on the practice of educational administration. *Review of Educational Research*, 70(1), 55–81.

Ryan, A. (2006). The role of social foundations in preparing teachers for culturally relevant practice. *Multicultural Education*, 13(3), 10–13.

Sheurich, J. J., & Young, M. D. (1997). Coloring epistemologies: Are our research epistemologies racially biased? *Educational Researcher*, 26(4), 4–16.

Shields, C., Larocque, L., & Oberg, S. (2002). A dialogue about race and ethnicity in education: Struggling to understand issues in cross-cultural leadership. *Journal of School Leadership*, 12(2), 116–137.

Theoharis, G. (2007). Social justice educational leaders and resistance: Toward a theory of Social justice leadership. *Educational Administration Quarterly*, 43, 221–258.

Tutwiler, S. W., deMarris, K., Gabbard, A. H., Konkol, P., Li, H., Medina, Y., ... Swain, A. (2013). Standards for academic and professional instruction in Foundations of Education, Educational Studies, and Educational Policy Studies (3rd ed., 2012). Draft presented to the educational community by the American Education Studies Association Committee on Academic Standards and Accreditation. *Educational Studies*, 49, 107–118.

Young, M., Mountford, M., & Skrla, L. (2006). Infusing gender and diversity issues into educational leadership programs. *Journal of Educational Administration*, 44(3), 264–277.

Chapter Two

Rocky Boats and Rainbows

Culturally Responsive Leadership from the Margin—An Autoethnography

Ann E. Lopez

INTRODUCTION

Increasing diversity in Canadian and American schools is a reality that cannot be ignored and presents significant challenges for teachers and educational leaders (Beachum & McCray, 2004). According to Statistics Canada (2005), by 2017 between 10 percent and 23 percent of Canada's population or roughly one out of every five people could be a member of a visible minority. Educational practices in schools do not reflect the demographic shifts taking place (Ryan, 2006). As this change occurs educational leaders are called on to create more equitable learning environments and adopt more culturally responsive and socially just approaches. In this changing environment, educational leaders and teachers must rethink their commitment to the preparation of all students (Beachum, 2011).

Parents from diverse communities are demanding that schools become more responsive to the educational needs of their children (Lopez, 2014). According to Gay (2010), schools need to become more interesting, engaging, and responsive to ethnically diverse students. This will not happen by chance. It requires focused action by educational leaders, continuous reflection and examination of their practices to unconditionally value the students they serve (Kea, Trent, & Davis, 2002; Lopez, 2011).

This chapter is an autoethnography of the researcher's lived experiences as a culturally responsive educational leader in two large, diverse, secondary schools in Southern Ontario, Canada. Autoethnography is a writing genre that "displays multiple layers of consciousness connecting the personal to the cultural" (Ellis & Bochner, 2000, p. 739), where the researcher becomes the phenomenon being studied (Ellis & Bochner, 2000).

As the researcher, one's personal narratives and reflections are used as a frame of reference within an autoethnographic methodological framework. This researcher's experience has been a journey of learning causing her to engage with new epistemologies through analysis of lived experiences as research data.

The chapter is organized in four sections. The first section explains the methodological approach of autoethnography, the second section looks at culturally responsive leadership, the third section represents the narrative through the use of the metaphors, and the fourth section highlights the insights gained and deconstructs culturally responsive educational leadership through the researcher's experiences and identity as a black racialized woman.

AUTOETHNOGRAPHY

Autoethnography is becoming an increasingly popular methodology in qualitative research. It is characterized by detailed and systematic examination of the researcher's lived experiences that illuminate deeper aspects of a culture by combining detailed field notes with the researcher's highly reflexive account of engaging in the research process (Allen-Collinson & Hockey, 2008). Autoethnography allows researchers to use their lived experiences within a particular culture to "look deeply at self-other interactions" (Ellis, 2004, p. 46) and also allows researchers to locate their personal experiences within the context of a culture and examine their experiences within that culture.

It validates the researcher's stories and narratives that might not necessarily be written about in other forms of academic writing. It is a form of writing characterized by "confessional tales" where the researcher's experiences become the object of the study and investigation (Ellis & Bochner, 2000). The thick documented accounts of one's lived experiences in autoethnographic research and the reflexivity that the researcher engages in give autoethnographies the capacity to be transformative to the researcher and to others.

Autoethnographic research challenges the canonical ways of doing research and treats research as a political, socially just and a socially conscious act (Adams & Holman Jones, 2008). Through autoethnography, researchers' personal experiences are validated and acknowledged and their subjectivity and emotionality accommodated (Ellis, Adams, & Bochner, 2010). The researcher/researched distinction that are common in traditional forms of research become blurred and this often times raises questions of validity in autoethnographies (Allen-Collinson & Hockey, 2008). Researchers who undertake autoethnogaphic studies argue that narratives derived from this kind of research cannot be measured against traditional forms of validity, reliability, and generalizability.

Lincoln and Guba (1985) argue instead for alternative ways of discussing the validity of research done using autoethnographic research methodology such as transferability and credibility, while others like Allen-Collinson and Hockey (2008) suggest that authenticity, congruence, and resonance might be more appropriate. This researcher believes that the autoethnographic research presented in this chapter will resonate with educational leaders in schools with large diverse student populations and educational leaders committed to social justice. The chapter examines the tensions and possibilities faced by educational leaders in diverse contexts and in particular those from racialized locations.

As a research methodology, autoethnography allowed the researcher to examine her lived experiences as a secondary school administrator, scholar, to make meaning of these experiences and theorize about one's practice (Dyson, 2007). Autoethnographies are thick descriptions of personal and interpersonal experiences that can make personal and social change possible for others (Ellis, 2002; Goodall, 2006).

The emotive and evocative qualities of this kind of research reaches deep into the researcher's experiences in a particular culture as the researcher relives, reflects, retells, and examines moments of critical encounters. Throughout the researcher's journey as a school leader, journals and reflective notes were kept to document her experiences. Engaging in this research has been transformative, allowing the researcher to construct new epistemologies about educational leadership as well as important skills to navigate as an educational leader from the margin—a black woman, immigrant and scholar. These experiences have created a new consciousness about leadership from an equity perspective and guided the researcher to a more purposeful praxis as a leader.

Autoethnographic research starts with descriptive narrative of events and activities that are unique to a particular culture and then moves into reflective analysis of these events and activities that allow the researcher to generate new insights and knowledge in the process (Duarte, 2007). In this study, the researcher draws from Atkinson (2002) notion of purging one's burden, Poulos (2008) notion of making sense of ourselves and experiences, and Pelias (2007) notion of using autoethnography to encourage personal responsibility and agency.

This study invites the readers to enter the researcher's world, using what they learn to reflect on their own lives (Ellis, 2004). In this study, the researcher writes about her experiences as a black, immigrant school administrator, and educational leader at Breezy Pines Secondary School and Riverview Secondary School (not the actual names)—two large diverse secondary schools in Southern Ontario, Canada. In conducting autoethnographic research, the researcher must be mindful of those within the culture that is being researched as well as those who might be impacted by the narratives that are produced.

Ellis (2007) refers to this as "relational ethics." Ellis suggests that when autoethnographic research is undertaken, researchers must be cognizant of "relational concerns" and as such might have to protect the privacy and safety of others by altering identifying characteristics such as circumstances, topics discussed, or characteristics like gender, race, name, place, and appearance. For that reason, pseudonyms are used and instances that might implicate others or create emotional or professional injury have been omitted or written in such a way to protect others from harm.

Autoethnographies make it possible for researchers to selectively and with hindsight write about epiphanies that come from or are made possible by being part of a culture (Ellis et al., 2010). Writing personal stories makes "witnessing" possible (Denzin, 2004; Ellis & Bochner, 2006). As witnesses, autoethnographers not only work with others to validate the meaning of their pain but also allow participants and readers to feel validated and better able to cope with their circumstances or be motivated to change their circumstances (Ellis et al., 2010).

The researcher was a school administrator and as such was part of the leadership culture of schools, where certain behaviors were expected of her both personally and professionally. The researcher brought to the role her multiple identities as a black, immigrant, mother, accented, and middle-class woman. Insights gained from examining these experiences have helped her to understand more effective ways of negotiating and navigating intense and difficult situations as an educational leader (Bochner, 1984).

"LITTLE BY LITTLE I WALKED FAR"— UNDERSTANDING CULTURALLY RESPONSIVE LEADERSHIP IN DIVERSE CONTEXTS

Using the Peruvian quote "Little by Little" is a metaphor to describe the new knowledge that the researcher gained on this journey as a culturally responsive and socially just school leader. The researcher learned to recognize the tensions along the way as deep moments of learning as well as strategies to navigate the complexities of schools. Her journey—from her roots in rural Jamaica to be-coming an educational leader in two large diverse secondary schools in Canada, championing the cause of those who have been excluded, oppressed, and marginalized—has been filled with moments of triumphs and challenges. The researcher uses the term be-coming to signal that her journey as an educational leader is ongoing, fluid, and changing.

Traditional theories of educational leadership, such as distributed leadership (Leithwood, 2001), do not explicitly address issues of social justice and equity in schools. The kind of educational leadership that the researcher advocates for is one that is socially just and culturally responsive (Beachum, 2011; Bogotch, 2005; Lopez, 2014; Ryan, 2010; Shields, 2010). Educational leaders who are socially just and culturally responsive take conscious actions to bring about change in their schools by ensuring that the curriculum is reflective of all learners and students, whose experiences have traditionally been excluded, are included. They seek to diversify teaching staffs by purposefully hiring teachers of color, engage in progressive and restorative disciplinary practices, and engage in meaningful collaboration with the communities that they serve.

Jean-Marie and Normore (2008) suggest that it is important for educators to tease out the work involved in a critical model of leadership so that others can learn from it. They suggest further that leadership for social justice must challenge social structures that privilege some and disadvantage others. Foster (1989, as cited in Jean-Marie & Normore, 2008) posits critical leadership as a continued analysis of what occurs in an organization with a commitment by those involved to engage in critical reflection and reevaluation of current practices.

Culturally responsive leaders must create a culture of learning that values parent participation and centers their funds of knowledge in teaching and learning (Moll, Amanti, Nedd, & Gonzalez, 2005). Culturally responsive leadership also involves the development of sociopolitical and critical consciousness that critiques cultural norms and institutions that produce and maintain social inequities (Ladson-Billings, 1995a, 1995b). In order for all students to experience success in school, teaching, learning and the school environment must include their experiences and be relevant to their lives (Lopez, 2011; Sullivan, 2010). Davis (2002) argues that the goal of culturally responsive leadership is to "devise mechanisms and environments for others to experience the freedom to become their best selves" (p. 5).

Beachum (2011) posits three key processes that must be present in culturally responsive leadership. These include (1) the development of emancipatory consciousness that focuses on educators' awareness of the history of societal inequities, (2) equitable insights that focus on the development of attitudes that promote inclusion throughout the school community, and (3) engagement in reflexive practices whereby educators critically examine the work they do.

This autoethnographic study allowed the researcher to engage in reflexivity as a school leader. Developing critical consciousness in educational leaders should be an important aspect of training programs that prepare educators for leadership roles in schools (Furman, 2012; Jean-Marie, Normore, & Brooks, 2009). In developing critical consciousness, educational leaders should be cognizant of the resistance they will face, develop strategies to cope, and the agency to improve the environment in which they work. As Ryan (2014) suggests, leadership practices are not always consistent with inclusion and socially just practices.

ROCKY BOATS AND RAINBOWS—BREEZY PINES SECONDARY SCHOOL AND RIVERVIEW SECONDARY SCHOOL

The metaphor "rocky boats and rainbows" represents the tensions, challenges, and celebrations in the researcher's journey of be-coming a culturally responsive and socially just school leader. She worked at Breezy Pines Secondary School and Riverview Secondary School, two large diverse secondary schools in Southern Ontario, Canada, for four years as a school leader. Both schools are located in very diverse communities that have seen tremendous growth in immigrant population and substantial demographic shifts over the past twenty years.

Breezy Pines Secondary School had just over 2,000 students and Riverview Secondary School had close to 600 students. The students in both schools were culturally, ethnically, economically, and racially diverse while the teaching staff was predominantly white. The teaching and administrative staff did not reflect the diversity of the schools' population or communities they serve. Both schools had white principals. The board had an equity and inclusive policy, but changes to the curriculum across the board were slow.

During the researcher's tenure as a school administrator at these schools, "zero-tolerance" was the stated disciplinary strategy in the schools. The Ontario *Safe Schools Act* and *Regulations* was passed in September 2001 by the Ontario Conservative government and was known as the "zero tolerance" policy. While some argued that the policies were "color blind," research indicated that it had disproportionate impact on racial minority students, particularly black students and students with disabilities (Daniel & Bondy, 2008). The *Safe Schools Act* took a hardline approach in dealing with student behavior and discipline. Under the *Safe Schools Act*, mandated mandatory suspensions and expulsions were given for infractions that involved the police regardless of the circumstances.

Opponents of the *Safe Schools Act* argued that students were suspended and expelled instead of receiving help. They argued that the *Safe School Act* criminalized students and student behavior thereby reducing students' life choices for employment and a productive life. Some called it the "gang recruitment act" as many students were thrown out of school with no future in sight.

Like Duarte (2007), the researcher's narrative is mixed. As a school leader, she was expected to uphold the *Safe Schools Act* and "zero tolerance" approach to discipline, even though she disagreed with the approach and the disciplinary strategies used in some instances. She saw first-hand each day the impact that "zero tolerance" had on marginalized students.

As a person of color and an educator who advocated for students marginalized by the education system, she experienced tremendous dissonance. As an administrator, she was expected to implement and enforce the *Safe School Policy and Regulation*. This caused moments of pain and agony, feelings of uncertainty, ambiguity, and frustration. On occasions she questioned being complicit in the marginalization of students of color as she watched students of color being harshly disciplined. At times, she felt unable or uncomfortable to confront the situation.

As a school administrator, she was expected to maintain discipline in the school and at times doled out lengthy suspensions to students even though she felt that the suspension would do more harm than good. She was challenged by the suspensions that were primarily for minority students who were sent to the office for minor infractions. In some instances, there was evidence that the disciplinary actions that some students themselves found were precipitated by the teachers' use and abuse of power. Many of the students who were disciplined were from low socioeconomic communities where their parents sometimes did not feel empowered to challenge the decisions made by the school.

In the researcher's early years as an administrator at Breezy Pines Secondary School, she struggled to find ways to challenge what she perceived as injustices to marginalized students. As Ryan (2014) suggests putting inclusive practices into place is not always easy and many practitioners struggle in their efforts to promote equitable practices. There were times when the researcher felt fearful of being viewed as soft on discipline and "going easy" on students of color because she is black. As the vice principal with the lowest seniority, she often remained silent. The principal at Breezy Pines made discipline and safety in the school her top priority, and the administrative team were expected to be good team players.

Breezy Pines Secondary School had a large South Asian and black student population, in addition to other ethnic groups. The researcher recalls one incident where a black student, whom she will call Donald, was being suspended for twenty days that would automatically lead to his expulsion from the school. Donald's parents were from Jamaica. Fearful that the parent would be angry about the length of the suspension, the principal asked the researcher to join her in the meeting with the parent. The principal wanted the researcher to join her since she was Jamaican, understood the Jamaican dialect, and would be able to calm the parent down should things "get out of hand."

The researcher recalls feeling extremely uncomfortable and conflicted about the meeting. She wanted to be a team player on the administrative team and support the decision of the principal, but felt that the punishment was too harsh for the infraction that was committed. She felt that more could have been done through restorative disciplinary practices to address the inappropriate behavior of the student. Her journal entry of that day reflected her anguish. She noted in her journal the number of suspensions and the large number of students of color that were being impacted. Veronica, the principal at Breezy Pines Secondary School, at staff meetings proudly announced how many expulsions were made and she was very proud of her record of expulsions from the school.

The researcher felt that Veronica used the zero tolerance policy to rid the school of students that were seen as problematic and these were often students of color. The researcher noted her discussions about her unease with a few teachers who were critical of her positions. She recalls how conflicted she felt. She was afraid of being seen as supporting the inappropriate behaviors of black students at the same time feeling hurt and pained by the process. The meeting was scheduled with Donald's mother who did not know ahead of time that Donald would be suspended from school for twenty days. She thought she was attending a meeting to discuss strategies to support her son who had found himself in a difficult situation. She was aware that there would be some consequence but not an expulsion.

The researcher felt extremely troubled and the incident marked a turning point for her with regard to making a conscious decision not to participate in the meeting with Veronica. The researcher walked into Veronica's office the morning of the meeting and told her that she was unable to sit in on the meeting because she felt uncomfortable. The researcher told Veronica that she should ask one of the other vice principals to attend the meeting with her.

The researcher was nervous and anxious about her decision as she walked into Veronica's office. She had the least seniority as a vice principal and in general, she did not feel supported by Veronica. Finding the political will to challenge Veronica was very difficult. After the meeting Veronica questioned the decision. The researcher had a critical friend and ally in the other two vice principals in the school. One was white and one was black. They shared the researcher's concern about the impact of the "zero tolerance" policy on the students of color in the school and supported the decision she made. Given the small number of administrators of color in the school at the time, having two administrators of color in the one school was rare.

Darlene, a black woman who had been a vice principal for a number of years, felt she was overlooked for promotion to principal despite her experience. Betty, who was white, was very supportive of racialized students and also expressed concerns about the impact of the disciplinary policy on students of color. This was a watershed moment for the researcher as an administrator. As she critically reflected on that moment, it signified for her a moment of both fear and courage, as well as a moment of agency and empowerment. As she reflects on that critical incident and her courage to act despite her fears, she realizes that it started her on a journey of thinking more deeply about her leadership practices and the kind of leader—socially just and culturally responsive—she wanted to become.

Her resolve and commitment to equity and culturally responsive practices as an educational leader was strengthened as she transferred to Riverview Secondary School after two years as an administrator at Breezy Pine Secondary. Frederick, the male white principal at Riverview Secondary, was generally supportive of her work and they had a good working relationship that she had not experienced with Veronica at Breezy Pine Secondary. The entry that she made in her journal after moving to Riverview Secondary School was a feeling of "deep resolve and less fear" as a school administrator. A journal entry read, "Breezy Pine has given me the courage to confront, disrupt, and advocate on behalf of students. I am better able to deal with my pain and fears of being a black woman in this role."

The researcher felt empowered moving to Riverview Secondary. She had worked hard on overcoming her fear of being seen as an administrator that was "soft on discipline" and a "supporter of racialized students." At Breezy Pine Secondary, she was worried about how she was "viewed and judged as a professional." It was difficult navigating the educational spaces given her identity and experiences where her knowledge was constantly challenged. At Breezy Pine Secondary, she also had friends among the teaching staff with whom she worked collaboratively to create more inclusive curricula which included, where possible, cultural events such as celebrations for Black History Month.

The student population at Riverview Secondary was a diverse mix of students of color, students from low-income homes, and students with special needs. Black boys were highly represented in the special education classes at Riverview Secondary. The overrepresentation of black students in special education classes was not surprising, as research has consistently shown that black boys tend to be in large numbers in special education classes (Blanchett, 2009). The disproportionate placement of children in special education classrooms has been persistent for African Americans (Gardner & Miranda, 2001), Latinos or Hispanics (Rostenberg, 2011), those learning English as a second language (Artiles & Klingner, 2006), and Native Americans (Ward, 2010) as cited in Codrington and Fairchild (2012).

Mahamed (2010) in her research on Somali Canadians noted that there was an overrepresentation in special education of poor, immigrant students of color, whose culture and language differ from that of English-speaking Canada. Canadian studies support the findings conducted by researchers in the United States. According to research conducted by the Toronto Board of Education (TDSB), at-risk students are increasingly defined along the lines of race. The research conducted in 2004–2005 found that "students born in the English speaking Caribbean (36%), Central/South America/Mexico (32%) and Eastern Africa (21%) tend to be more highly at-risk than the average" (Brown, 2006, p. 27).

At Riverview, the researcher noticed a distinct authoritarian tone by some teachers when dealing with student discipline. The teaching staff at Riverview Secondary similar to Breezy Pine Secondary was primarily white and not reflective of the student population. There were constant complaints from some teachers about the behavior of students. The office at Riverview Secondary was always filled with students to be disciplined for one reason or another. The local police was a constant presence in the school and had the support of the outgoing vice principal, Mr. Brown, who told the researcher, as he was handing over details of students' files to her, "you will be fine, they are all thugs, the police will be your best friend."

The journal entry the researcher made that day noted the "sinking feeling in her stomach" after her conversation with Mr. Brown and her resolve "to ignore his suggestion"; "I am not Mr. Brown, I don't want to treat these children like Mr. Brown, this will not be easy," she noted in her journal. As she reflects on her journal entry and that critical moment, she feared the challenges ahead of her at Riverview, but she felt stronger knowing that she had a principal who supported her and she was more committed given her experience at Breezy Point Secondary.

At Riverview Secondary, there was a constant bevy of students in the office to be disciplined for minor infractions. The contact room that supported students who were having difficulties in class also had a constant flow. Some teachers sent students to the office to be disciplined with suggestions on the outcome they wanted and became enraged when the researcher did not comply with their suggestions. The researcher felt overwhelmed, yet hopeful that she could make a difference at Riverview Secondary.

Her approach to discipline at Riverview was to listen to the students, make contact with parents, support teachers in their classroom efforts, and use suspension only as a last resort or in circumstances when suspension was mandated. Some teachers openly criticized her approach to discipline. Some of the students at Riverview Secondary were challenging behaviorally and many of them had never experienced success in their schooling. As a result, some of these students had lost hope in the education process.

The researcher was viewed as an outsider at the school. Many of the teachers and teaching assistants had been there for a long time and there was low turnover among the staff. The researcher's leadership was oftentimes questioned by the predominantly white teaching staff some of whom had only been teaching for a short period of time, yet they felt confident to challenge her professional knowledge despite her years of teaching and administrative experience. Ellis (1999) suggests that structures in the Canadian labor force position professionals especially those from minority backgrounds as "disentitled" and de-skilled.

Some teachers questioned the researcher's knowledge of special education, assessment, and evaluation resisting any suggestions for improvement in their pedagogy (Lopez, 2013). As the researcher faced resistance at Riverview Secondary, she did not feel the same level of anxiety that she felt at Breezy Pines Secondary. From her journey at Breezy Pines, she learned to deal with resistance and draw on critical friends for support. Sagor (2000) suggests that by forming groups of "critical friends," educators can assist one another through listening, questioning, and collaboration.

One afternoon while a school leadership meeting was in progress, there was knock on the door of the room that the meeting was being held in. It was Mr. Dixon, a white male teacher who had been at the school for some time. Mr. Dixon complained that there was a group of boys making noise in the school. He indicated that the researcher needed to leave the meeting and accompany him to get the boys out of the school. Riverview Secondary had a policy of loitering after school hours requiring students to vacate the building at the end of the school day. Mr. Dixon insisted that the researcher instruct the students to leave the school premises.

When the two administrators arrived, it was a group of about eight black boys waiting for the transit, playing music, and talking among themselves. The weather outside was −20 degrees Celsius with a wind chill. The students told the researcher that it was very cold outside and that was the reason they were waiting inside for the city bus to arrive. The researcher told them to be a little quieter while they waited and left. It was the end of the day, classes were not in progress, and she saw no harm in what they were doing.

Mr. Dixon became agitated and angry at her approach and suggested that she was the problem for the lack of discipline at Riverview and stormed away. The researcher returned to the meeting and late that evening made a journal note. In her journal, she noted. "Mr. Dixon is angry again … he yelled at me in my office last week because I did not suspend … whom he reported to the office for opposition to authority … I wait to see how much this incident will escalate … he continues to disrespect me and the students." As the researcher reflected on this episode, and Mr. Dixon, she can only describe his actions toward the students and herself as racist.

Throughout researcher's time at Riverview Secondary, she watched Mr. Dixon become enraged at students of color for minor infractions such as not taking off their hats promptly enough upon his request. In one instance, she watched Mr. Dixon chase after a student who was trying to leave the building.

Challenging racism in schools oftentimes create disagreements, resentment, and resistance. Like Cho (2011), the researcher was not fully prepared as a racial minority to traverse the difficult and tension-filled conversations about race that often occur in schools. She had not anticipated the feelings of pain and trauma that such moments evoke. There were times she felt responsible to educate teachers about the impact of racism on students and times she felt worn down by the racist attitudes toward her from some staff members.

Confronting racism has always been a part of her existence growing up on an island that was once inhabited by slaves and the vestiges of colonialism. She came of age during a time of great political upheaval and change in Jamaica and in the broader sphere of international development, where the Civil Rights Movement sparked global awareness of the devastating consequences of disenfranchisement, oppression, and racism.

From this early beginning, the act of becoming a critical thinker was set in motion for life. The strong winds of social change and the demand for independence in Jamaica during the 1960s permeated Jamaica's history and engendered a climate of proactivism in her. As the beneficiary of free public education that allowed her to attend the island's only university, where previously only the elite had access, she is deeply committed to ensuring that all children have access to a just and equitable education, regardless of their location in the world. She gained access to this education as a result of the transformative work of radical leaders who were "not afraid to confront, to listen, to see the world transformed" (Friere, 1970/1993, p. 21).

There were very few teachers of color at Riverview. With a large diverse student population, she felt that it was important to have teachers who represented the diversity of the students. The students needed to see more positive role models and the school needed to hire more teachers of color. More than half of the students at Riverview Secondary were students of color. Increasing the number of teachers of color provided real-life examples to diverse students that teaching is a possibility for them (Bireda & Chait, 2011). We know from research that racialized students perform better when they have teachers of color in the school.

While many teachers can provide effective pedagogy and support to diverse students, research has shown that when teachers of color are in the classroom, students of color experience increasing academic achievement (Dee, 2004). The white principal at Riverview was supportive of increasing the diversity among the teaching staff and over the course of two years hired five teachers of color. The researcher reflecting on the actions to increase the diversity in the teaching staff made a conscious decision not to use the term "qualified" to describe teachers of color who were hired. Often times when conscious decisions are made to hire people of color, the term "qualified" is sometimes used to justify the hiring, which feeds into the notion that people of color are not as qualified and need special status.

Some members of the teaching staff became upset at the number of teachers of color who were hired and suggested that it was "reverse racism" and openly complained that the school should be hiring the most "qualified" teachers and not just seek to hire teachers of color suggesting that teachers of color are not automatically thought to be as qualified as their white counterparts. The researcher has never heard anyone say that they hired the most "qualified" white teacher. It is the assumption that when a white teacher is hired they are qualified.

Mrs. Dime, who taught languages at Riverview, decided that she would be the spokesperson for those on staff who had concerns about the number of teachers of color that were hired and wanted a friendly chat to discuss her concerns. In the meeting, the researcher asked Mrs. Dime why she thought the teachers who were hired were not "qualified." She told me that she "just wanted to make sure that we were not lowering standards." The researcher suggested to Mrs. Dime that she had nothing to worry about and reminded her that she has never heard anyone suggest that we need to make sure that we hire the most qualified "white" teacher.

Mrs. Dime was not angry and in fact thought that she was doing a good deed. We had a good conversation and the researcher shared some culturally responsive resources with Ms. Dime. The two even engaged in conversations about race and racism in the school and Canada as a whole. The researcher took the opportunity to invite Mrs. Dime to dialogue more around issues that were of concern to her. It was important that the researcher did not alienate her. If change is to take place in the lives of diverse students, then conscious actions must be taken to build relationships with those who are willing to engage in dialogue.

One of the researcher's aspirations at Riverview was to make greater connections with the parents in the community. She made a commitment to inform parents of school processes and provided support where possible in navigating the vast amount of information that can sometimes come from the school. She also supported parents in understanding their rights under the *Education Act* that governs education in Ontario to understand that they do not have to accept the suggestions of guidance counselors when it comes to the future education of their children. Revisiting her journal notes and reflecting on her experiences has caused her to think about her leadership practices. As the researcher writes this autoethnography it causes her to reflect on what she needs to learn about navigating the educational leadership terrain.

PADDLING IN ROUGH WATERS AND STAYING AFLOAT—LEARNINGS AND INSIGHTS

Through this study, the researcher has developed a better understanding of how to navigate complex and challenging school environments and face challenging issues. Even though her journey was rocky at times, and she "paddled in rough waters" a metaphor for her journey, she stayed afloat because of the support of critical friends and a commitment not to give up even when the journey became lonely.

She uses this metaphor to guide the recounting and retelling of her experiences and personal journey (Dyson, 2007). She has gained a deeper understanding of how to engage in culturally responsive and socially just leadership as a woman of color. There were moments she felt powerless and afraid to act, but grew stronger in her own sense of agency and commitment. Becoming a culturally responsive leader is a process that involves continuous learning and unlearning, that raises complex questions about the role and responsibilities of school leaders. This tension between learning and unlearning, as well as realigning one's professional identity between old and new, is an important insight she learned on this journey.

Reflecting on this research journey, she draws on Dyson (2007) notion of the research journey being layered and told through the use of metaphors. She sees her research journey as having three layers: (1) The first layer was a pain-filled journey that can be characterized as "rocky boats." Through authoethnography the researcher had to relive many of the negative experiences she encountered (Atkinson, 2002). (2) The researcher had to make sense of these experiences (Poulos, 2008), which caused her to theorize and gain new understandings, which helped her to stay afloat. (3) The third layer is the researcher's sense of personal responsibility and agency (Pelias, 2007) and imagining possibilities like rainbows that appear after a storm.

Navigating School Contexts and Spaces. Through this journey, the researcher has gained insights on how school leaders from marginalized groups can navigate school spaces occupied by predominantly white bodies. As she reflects on this journey, she has learned how to navigate the minefields of the social contexts of schools. By navigating, she means understanding the context, finding spaces and situations to act, understanding when to be patient, like a ship sailing on rough seas, looking for calm channels, avoiding rocks, keeping one's eyes on the prize, and their hands on the wheel.

She learned to engage in purposeful praxis and agency taking joy from small victories, seek out allies and critical friends, develop cross-cultural understanding, build bridges with parents and families, create space to include the voices of parents and students in the process, build relationships, and most importantly feel a sense of empowerment that despite the challenges work toward change. This important work cannot be done alone, it is important that culturally responsive leaders build communities of practice and learn with others.

CONCLUSION

The researcher embarked on this study to enlighten her own understanding of culturally responsive and socially just educational leadership. In reflecting on the journey and using autoethnography as the framework, she has been able to understand more deeply, what it means to be a racialized school leader and an immigrant in a context where the majority of the teaching, administrative, and support staff are white. Furthermore, she understands how her educational philosophy is not shared nor is her knowledge valued. It is clear to her how the values of the dominant group are privileged and meritocracy is advocated instead of equity. These experiences have caused the researcher to find inner strength.

The researcher used the tools of metaphor and narrative to examine, reflect, and conceptualize her journey as a school leader (Dyson, 2007). This process has helped her to imagine possibilities for culturally responsive, socially just, and equitable leadership. Imagining is important in the formation of self-identity within a community of practice. It is a way of looking at ourselves and our situations with new eyes and being aware of multiple ways that we interpret our lives (Wagner, 1998).

This study has implications for K–12 school leadership and others who do scholarly work about leadership. The researcher has not captured all of the moments in this journey; it is still incomplete. As a research methodology, autoethnography has provided her with the space to critically reflect on her experiences, forging new understandings about schools as organizations.

Listening to the voices of leaders who engage in culturally responsive practices will help to facilitate, unpack, and problematize institutional policies that are ingrained in leadership knowledge production (Arnold & Brooks, 2013). It has been a transformative experience with new knowledge and insights gained on culturally responsive and socially just leadership practices. As a result of these experiences, the researcher now approaches educational leadership differently, less as a "performer" dancing to the beats of the system, wrapped in fear, and more as a conscious critical scrutinizer seeking out opportunities to create change.

Dyson (2007) suggests the landscape of transformation as he describes it, allowing us to be in a state of becoming. He argues that autoethnography facilitates transformational writing, "The writing of transforming autoethnography, containing multiple payer of consciousness, connecting the personal to the cultural and embracing the power of metaphor, has the potential to move both the author and the readers into the landscape of transformation" (p. 10). As the researcher embarks on different roads in this journey as an educator, she begins with a new consciousness gained from this work imagining rainbows in the distance.

REFERENCES

Adams, T. E. & Holman Jones, S. (2008). Autoethnography is queer. In N. K. Denzin, Y. Lincoln, & L. T. Smith (Eds.), *Handbook of critical and indigenous methodologies* (pp. 373–390). Thousand Oaks, CA: Sage.

Allen-Collinson, J., & Hockey, J. (2008). Autoethnography as "valid" methodology? A study of disrupted identity narratives. *The International Journal of Interdisciplinary Social Sciences*, 3(6), 209–217.

Arnold, N. W., & Brooks, J. S. (2013). Getting churched and being schooled making meaning of leadership practice. *Journal of Cases in Educational Leadership*, 16(2), 44–53.

Artiles, A. J., & Klingner, J. K. (2006). Forging a knowledge base on English language learners with special needs: Theoretical, population, and technical issues. *Teachers College Record*, 108(11), 2187–2194. doi:10.1111/j.1467-9620.2006.00778.x

Atkinson, R. (2002). The life story interview as a bridge in narrative inquiry. In D. Jean Clandinin (Ed.), *Handbook of narrative inquiry* (pp. 224–245). Thousand Oaks, CA: Sage.

Beachum, F. (2011). Culturally relevant leadership for complex 21st century school contexts. In F. English (Ed.), *The Sage handbook of educational leadership* (4th ed., pp. 27–35). Thousand Oaks, CA: Sage Publications.

Beachum, F. D., & McCray, C. R. (2004). Cultural collision in urban schools. *Current Issues in Education*, 7(5). Retrieved from http://cie.asu.edu/volume7/number5/

Bireda, S., & Chait, R. (2011). Increasing teacher diversity: Strategies to improve teacher workforce. Retrieved from https://cdn.americanprogress.org/wp-content/uploads/issues/2011/11/pdf/chait_diversity.pdf

Blanchett, W. J. (2009). A retrospective examination of urban education: From brown to the resegregation of African Americans in special education—It is time to "go for broke." *Urban Education*, 44(4), 370–388.

Bogotch, I. (2005). *Social justice as an educational construct: Problems and possibilities*. Paper presented at the Annual Meeting of the University Council of Educational Administration, Nashville, TN.

Bochner, A. P. (1984). The functions of human communication in interpersonal bonding. In C. C. Arnold & J. W. Bowers (Eds.), *Handbook of rhetorical and communication theory* (pp. 544–621). Boston: Allyn and Bacon.

Brown, R. S. (2006). *TDSB secondary student success indicators, 2004–2005*. Toronto, Canada: Toronto District School Board, Organizational Development Department, Research and Information Services.

Cho, H. (2011). Lessons learned: Teaching the race concept in the college classroom. *Multicultural Perspectives*, 13(1), 36–41.

Codrington, J., & Fairchild, H. H. (2012). Special education and the mis-education of African American children: A call to action. Washington, DC: The Association of Black Psychologists.

Daniel, Y., & Bondy, B. (2008). Safe schools in Ontario and Zero tolerance: Policy, program and practices in Ontario. *Canadian Journal of Educational Administration and Policy*, (70), 1–20. Retrieved from http://files.eric.ed.gov/fulltext/EJ806990/pdf

Davis, D. M. (2002). Toward democratic education: The importance of culturally responsive leadership in 21st Century schools. *Trotter Review*, 14(1). Retrieved from http://scholarworks.umb.edu/trotter_Review/vol14/ss/1/3

Dee, T. (2004). Teachers, race and student achievement in a randomized experiment The. *Review of Economics and Statistics*, 86(1), 195–210.

Denzin, N. K. (2004). The war on culture, the war on truth. *Cultural Studies -Critical Methodologies*, 4(2), 137–142.

Duarte, F. (2007). Using autoethnography in the scholarship of teaching and learning: Reflective practice from the 'other side of the mirror.' *International Journal for the Scholarship of Teaching and Learning*, 1(2), 1–11. Retrieved from http://www.georgiasouthrn.edu/ijstol

Dyson, M. (2007). My story in a profession of stories: Auto ethnography—An empowering methodology for educators. *Australian Journal Teacher Education*, 32(1), 36–48.

Ellis, S. N. (1999). *A multilayer evaluation of the responsive classroom approach.* Retrieved from http://www.responsive%20classroom.org/about.research.html

Ellis, C. (2002). Being real: Moving inward toward social change. *Qualitative Studies in Education*, 15(4), 399–406.

Ellis, C. (2004). *The ethnographic: A methodological novel about autoethnography.* Walnut Creek, CA: AltaMira Press.

Ellis, C. (2007). Telling secrets, revealing lives: Relational ethics in research with intimate others. *Qualitative Inquiry*, 13(1), 3–29.

Ellis, C., Adams, T. E., & Bochner, A. P. (2010). Autoethnography: An overview. *Forum Qualitative Social Research*, 12(1), Art 10. Retrieved from http://nbn-resolving.de/urn:nbnde:0114fqs1101108

Ellis, C., & Bochner, A. (2000). Autoethnography, personal narrative, reflexivity: Researcher as subject. In N. Denzin & Y. Lincoln (Eds.), *Sage handbook of qualitative research* (2nd ed., pp. 733–768). Thousand Oaks, CA: Sage.

Ellis, C., & Bochner, P. (2006). Analyzing analytic autoethnography: An autopsy. *Journal of Contemporary Ethnography*, 35(4), 429–449.

Foster, W. F. (1989). Towards a critical practice of leadership. In J. Smyth (Ed.), *Critical prospectus on educational leadership*. London: The Falmer Press.

Friere, P. (1970/1993). *Pedagogy of the oppressed*. New York: New York Continuum International.

Furman, G. (2012). Social justice leadership as praxis: Developing capacities through preparation programs. *Educational Administration Quarterly*, 48(92), 191–229.

Gay, G. (2010). *Culturally responsive teaching: Theory, research, and practice* (2nd ed.). New York: Teachers College Press.

Gardner, R. I., II, & Miranda, A. H. (2001). Improving outcomes for urban African American students. *Journal of Negro Education*, 70(4), 255–263. doi:10. 2307/3211278

Goodall, B. H. L. (2006). *A need to know: The clandestine history of a CIA family*. Walnut Creek, CA: Left Coast Press.

Jean-Marie, G., & Normore, A. H. (2008). A repository of hope for social justice. Black women leaders at historically Black colleges and universities. In A. Normore (Ed.), *Leadership for social justice: Promoting equity and excellence through inquiry and reflection practice* (pp. 3–35). Charlotte, NC: Information Age.

Jean-Marie, G., Normore, A. H., & Brooks, J. S. (2009). Leadership for social justice: Preparing 21st century school leaders for a new social order. *Journal of Research on Leadership Education*, 4(1), 1–31.

Kea, C. D., Trent, S. C., & Davis, C. P. (2002). African American student teachers' preparations about preparedness to teach students from culturally and linguistically diverse backgrounds. *Multiple Perspectives*, 4(1), 18–25.

Ladson-Billings, G. (1995a). But that's just good teaching. The case for culturally relevant pedagogy. *Theory into Practice*, 34(3), 159–165.

Ladson-Billings, G. (1995b). Toward a theory of culturally relevant pedagogy. *American Educational Research Journal*, 32(3), 465–491.

Leithwood, K. (2001). School leadership in the context of accountability policies. *International Journal of Leadership in Education*, 4(3), 217–236.

Lincoln, Y., & Guba, E. (1985). *Naturalistic inquiry*. Beverly Hills, CA: Sage Publications.

Lopez, A. E. (2011). Culturally relevant pedagogy and critical literacy in diverse English classrooms: Case study of a secondary English teacher's activism and agency. *English Teaching: Practice and Critique*, 10(4), 75–93.

Lopez, A. E. (2013). Embedding and sustaining equitable practices in teachers' everyday work: A framework for critical action. *Teaching & Learning*, 7(3), 1–15.

Lopez, A. E. (2014). Reconceptualising teacher leadership through curriculum inquiry in pursuit of social justice: Case study from the Canadian context. In I. Bogotch & C. Shields (Eds.), *International handbook of educational leadership and social (in) justice* (pp. 465–484). New York, NY. Springer Dordrecht Heidelberg.

Mahamed, F. (2010). There is no choice: Examining Somali parents' experience with special education. Master's Thesis. Retrieved from https://tspace.library.utoronto.ca/bitstream/1807/24231/1/Mahamed_Fowzia_20103_MA_thesis.pdf

Moll, L., Amanti, C., Nedd, D., & Gonzalez, N. (Eds.). (2005). *Funds of knowledge: Theorizing practices in households, communities and classrooms*. Mahwah, NJ: Lawrence Erlbaum.

Pelias, R. J. (2007). Jamhead, girlymen, and the pleasure of violence. *Qualitative Inquiry*, 13(7), 945–959.

Poulos, C. N. (2008). *Accidental ethnography: An inquiry into family secrecy*. Walnut Creek, CA: Left Coast Press.

Rostenberg, D. (2011). *Disproportionate representation of Hispanic students in Arizona's special education programs*. Doctoral Dissertation. Available from Dissertation Abstracts International Section A, 71. EBSCOhost.

Ryan, J. (2006). Inclusive leadership. San Francisco, CA: Jossey-Bass.

Ryan, J. (2010). Establishing inclusion in new school: The role of principal leadership. *Exceptionality Education International*, 20(2), 6–24.

Ryan, J. (2014). Promoting inclusive leadership in diverse schools. In I. Bogotch & C. Shields (Eds.), *International handbook of educational leadership and social (in) justice* (pp. 465–484). New York, NY: Springer Dordrecht Heidelberg.

Sagor, S. (2000). *The action research guidebook: A four-stage process for educators and school*. Thousand Islands, CA: Corwin.

Shields, C. (2010). Transformative leadership: Working for equity in diverse contexts. *Educational Administration Quarterly*, 46(4), 558–589.

Statistics Canada. (2005). Retrieved from http://www.statcan.gc.ca/daily-/050322/dq050322b eng.htm

Sullivan, J. A. (2010). *Making a difference: A study of the perceptions, classroom management, and instructional practices of teachers who use culturally responsive strategies to teach African American adolescent male students.* Doctoral Dissertation. Available from Abstracts International Section A, 71, Retrieved from EBSCOhost.

Wagner, B. J. (1998). *Educational drama and language arts: What research shows.* Portsmouth NH: Heinemann.

Ward, S. M. (2010). *Bridging the gap: Documenting Clinton school district's (CSD's) journey addressing racial/ethnic disproportion in special education.* Doctoral Dissertation. Available from ProQuest Information & Learning. Dissertation Abstracts International Section A: Humanities and Social Sciences, 70(8). 2010-99030-015.

Chapter Three

Change Your School, Change the World

The Role of School Leaders in Implementing Schoolwide Restorative Justice and Relational Pedagogies

Martha Brown and Katherine Evans

INTRODUCTION

This chapter is written with the hope of inspiring school leaders to create more just and equitable schools by implementing schoolwide restorative justice—a reform capable of transforming schools into places where relationships are a priority and where all people in the school community are empowered to act in the best interests of themselves and each other. We believe the values, theories, and practices of restorative justice in education explained in this chapter will provide school leaders with a rationale for rejecting discriminatory zero tolerance discipline policies and considering instead schoolwide restorative justice and relational pedagogies that create caring school communities that value relationships, facilitate student learning, and promote more just ways of resolving conflict and solving problems.

We start by critiquing zero tolerance school disciplinary practices that disproportionately affect students of color and then introduce Restorative Justice in Education (RJE) as not only a viable alternative to zero tolerance, but more importantly, as a way to transform school culture and how people in school relate to each other on a daily basis. Within the framework of change theory, we discuss the importance of visionary leadership in both creating relational trust across the school community and in empowering teachers, students, parents, and community members to provide input so that schoolwide change is successful and sustainable. Finally, we offer practical suggestions on how to create a more restorative ethos in schools and provide recommendations on how school leaders can learn more about the transformative potential of restorative justice.

ZERO TOLERANCE: A DISASTROUS FAILURE

Since the 1980s, a growing fear of juvenile violence and tough-on-crime political rhetoric has led to the widespread implementation of harshly punitive school disciplinary policies commonly known as zero tolerance (Browne-Dianis, 2011; Kennedy-Lewis, 2013; Simon, 2007). While zero tolerance policies were intended to ensure school safety, they have resulted in the exclusion of hundreds of thousands of students, most of whom are black and brown boys who are easily absorbed by the prison industrial complex and who become part of what is commonly referred to as the school to prison pipeline, a phenomenon criticized as discriminatory, unjust, and undemocratic (Cassella, 2003; Davis, 2012; Gillborn, 2010; Hoffman, 2014; Kennedy-Lewis, 2013; Skiba, Arrendondo, & Rausch, 2014).

The criminalization of a myriad of student behaviors has led to the merging of the educational and penal systems to produce the collapse of progressive education and the implementation of a highly authoritarian, mechanistic, and scientific model of education (Hirschfield, 2008; Kliebard, 2009; Nguyen, 2013; Simon, 2007).

The physical environment of many schools, particularly those in urban settings, has changed such that they resemble correctional institutions more so than institutions of learning; visitor sign-ins, barbed-wire fencing, security and surveillance technologies, drug sweeps, locker searches, metal detectors, drug and weapon-sniffing dogs, and armed school resource officers (SROs) are now commonplace (Kupchik, 2010; Simon, 2007). These fortress tactics, as Simon calls them, and other tools and philosophies of the criminal justice system dominate school environments, framing nonwhite students as criminals.

Rather than making schools safer and minimizing violence, zero tolerance policies have shifted the responsibility for solving problems from the schools to the criminal justice system, writing off the student in an attempt to intimidate the group (Ladson-Billings, 2001; Teske, 2011). Problems, conflicts, and behaviors previously handled by school administrators and counselors are instead referred to school police and juvenile justice officials, feeding the school to prison pipeline that has been flowing and growing for the past several decades (Hulac, Terrell, Vining, & Berstein, 2011; Skiba et al., 2014).

The American Psychological Association Zero Tolerance Task Force (2008) concluded that zero tolerance policies, as currently implemented, fail

to achieve the goals of an effective system of school discipline and are counter to healthy child and adolescent development. Zero tolerance policies do
not promote or teach desirable behaviors, as they encourage more aggressive
behavior, instigate rebellion and defiance, cease to be punishing, and reward
some students who really do not want to be in school by suspending them
(Hoffman, 2014; Hulac et al., 2011; Jones, 2013; Skiba, 2001).

Advanced by an overemphasis on standardized test scores and a de-
emphasis on relationships and healthy school cultures, school activity is often
organized around the tasks of classifying students and forcing out the lowest
class of performers, often for behavioral reasons (Brown, 2007; Dohrn, 2001;
Gonzalez, 2012; Rodriquez, 2013). Labeling students as delinquents or future
prisoners in need of exclusion or coercive control creates a self-fulfilling
prophecy (Moore, 2011; Zembroski, 2011), while racial stereotypes in the
media continually portray black males as unsalvageable, making their future
role as prisoners almost inevitable (Davis, 2012; Hirschfield, 2008).

If the effectiveness of any disciplinary system is determined by how it
teaches students to solve problems and conflicts without resorting to disruption and violence, then zero tolerance policies have been proven to be a
disastrous failure (Reyes, 2006; Skiba et al., 2014; Skiba & Peterson, 2000).
What has been highly effective in cultivating positive school environments,
creating just schools, and decreasing challenging or disruptive student behavior is restorative justice (Hopkins, 2004; Morrison, 2007; Sellman, Cremin, &
McCluskey, 2013).

RESTORATIVE JUSTICE IN EDUCATION:
A TRANSFORMATIVE REFORM

Although restorative justice (RJ) first appeared in the criminal justice system,
schools around the United States and the world have been applying restorative justice principles and processes since the 1990s (Riestenberg, 2012).
Morrison (2007) defines RJ as both a process and a set of values that is about
"addressing basic social and emotional needs of individuals and communities, particularly in the context of responding to harmful behavior to oneself
and others" (p. 73).

RJE reflects restorative justice philosophy, values, theory, and practices
as applied and modified for explicit use in the school environment. RJE
attempts to facilitate healthy school relationships, address challenging student behavior, and foster positive classroom environments (Evans & Lester,
2013; Vaandering, 2010). After conducting a review of the literature, Evans
and Lester concluded that restorative justice in education is about (1) meeting needs, (2) providing accountability and support, (3) making things

right, (4) viewing conflict as a learning opportunity, (5) building healthy learning communities, (6) restoring relationships, and (7) addressing power imbalances.

Restorative values are "about healing rather than hurting, moral learning, community participation and community caring, respectful dialogue, forgiveness, responsibility, apology, and making amends" (Morrison, 2007, p. 75). These values include but are not limited to empowerment, honesty, respect, engagement, compassion, empathy, inclusion, responsibility, mutual care, open-mindedness, and humility (Morrison, 2007; Pranis, 2007). Restorative justice intentionally works from a value-based philosophy that ultimately "grounds and enhances our notions of freedom, democracy, and community" (Morrison, 2007, p. 76) and emphasizes interconnectedness and relationship building (Pranis, 2005; Zehr, 2002).

Restorative justice in education is applied through practices and processes that create positive and caring school cultures and respond to situations where harm has been committed. Hopkins (2011) refers to the latter as a sharp end response to specific behaviors; however, researchers and practitioners have determined that using restorative approaches strictly as a sharp end response to harm is far less effective than a schoolwide approach.

When RJE is embraced schoolwide, there is a focus on building strong, supportive, and healthy relationships between all members of the school community; restorative processes facilitate active listening and mindful speaking; restorative language is used throughout the building; and restorative and relational pedagogies, such as circles, are used in classrooms to build community, deliver content, and solve problems (Hopkins, 2004, 2011; Morrison, 2007; Riestenberg, 2012).

Responsive Restorative Responses. In the early years of RJE implementation (and still in many schools today), restorative approaches were used only *after* a harm had been committed and in response to some offense, incident, or rule violation. In the restorative paradigm, accountability is redefined whereby the person who committed the harm is held directly accountable for repairing the harm and making things right as much as possible, often in lieu of or alongside a punitive sanction.

Likewise, the person(s) harmed has the opportunity to state what is needed to heal and move forward. Considering that many harms affect other members of the school community, including teachers and other students, community members also participate in processes that focus on restoring broken relationships, and support is provided to all involved so that the issue is resolved in ways that allow everyone to be heard and better understood (Hopkins, 2011; Stutzman Amstutz & Mullet, 2005; Zehr, 2002). The person who committed harm is then reintegrated into his or her school or classroom community while in the process of or after meeting the agreed upon obligations for reparation (Claassen & Claassen, 2008; Stutzman Amstutz & Mullet, 2005).

Unlike exclusionary discipline policies that carry the stigmatizing shame that produces additional bad behavior and isolation, restorative approaches allow the person who committed harm to learn resiliency and to increase his or her self-awareness, self-management, social awareness, and relationship-building skills (Goleman, 1995; Morrison, 2007).

Preventative Restorative Approaches. When RJE is universally applied across all school environments, and various restorative approaches and relational pedagogies are used daily, people in schools grow to trust and respect each other and are therefore less apt to speak and act in ways that cause harm to others. In these schools, staff is trained to use restorative language, make relationships with students and with each other a priority, and work together to create a healthy and supportive community that discourages harmful behavior and prevents violence (Hopkins, 2004, 2011; Morrison, 2006, 2007; Morrison & Vaandering, 2012; Riestenberg, 2012).

Adopting schoolwide restorative approaches (SWRAs) strengthens the social ties of youth to people and institutions much more so that restorative practices narrowly focus on a particular set of disciplinary problems (Hopkins, 2004; Karp & Breslin, 2001; Morrison, 2007; Morrison & Vaandering, 2012). The latest iteration of RJE encourages applying restorative justice values and practices in the form of relational pedagogy and speaking restoratively across the entire school environment. This links thinking and acting restoratively to students' ability to develop a sense of self-efficacy and self-awareness as restorative approaches offer a flexible, adaptable continuum of informal and formal responses for developing relationships and responding to harm (Collaborative for Academic and Social Emotional Learning, n.d.; Hopkins, 2011; Macready, 2009; Riestenberg, 2012).

Relational and Restorative Pedagogy. Hopkins (2011) defines relational and restorative pedagogy as a method of teaching based on the notion of developing relationships and connections with the self, with others, and with the curriculum. Relational pedagogy involves using language that "maintains connection, respect, and mutual understanding" and when disconnection occurs, "then reconnection is encouraged at the earliest possible opportunity, using restorative processes" (Hopkins, 2011, p. 15).

Relational and restorative pedagogy requires teachers to use different assessments and evaluations, alternative planning, and intentional objectives that teach and model appropriate ways of relating to self and others by fostering emotional intelligence (Goleman, 1995; Hopkins, 2011). RJE aligns with Social Emotional Learning (SEL) competencies (CASEL, n.d.); in table 3.1 we juxtapose the outcomes of restorative approaches to SEL competencies to more clearly illustrate this connection.

Table 3.1   Outcomes of Restorative Approaches and Social Emotional Learning Competencies

Restorative Approaches...	SEL Competency
Encourage dialogue between all those involved or affected by a situation, incident, or event	Relationship skills Self-management
Appreciate and acknowledge the differing views and perspectives that dialogue encourages	Social awareness Self-awareness
Recognize that what people do and say is influenced by their thoughts, beliefs, feelings, and unmet needs	Self-awareness
Take these thoughts, beliefs, feelings, and unmet needs into consideration in finding ways forward when planning, problem solving, or resolving conflicts	Self-management Social awareness Relationship skills
Believe that the people who have the problem are the ones best suited to find their own answers and solutions	Responsible decision making
Trust in the capacity of people to know how to find their own ways forward and the importance of letting them do this	Self-management Responsible decision making

Note: Adapted from Hopkins (2004, p. 180) and CASEL (n.d.).

In her book, *Circle in the Square: Building Community and Repairing Harm in School*, Riestenberg (2012) related anecdotes from teachers and administrators who implemented restorative measures and relational pedagogies throughout Minnesota schools. Teachers shared stories of how they used circles to deliver lessons, assessed student learning, built communities of trust in their classrooms, and solved problems when they occurred.

Teachers who used restorative circles in their classrooms on a regular basis facilitated students' social emotional competencies of self-awareness, self-management, social awareness, responsible decision-making, and relationship skills. The experiences shared by these teachers illustrate how SEL and restorative approaches can easily be incorporated into daily instructional practices without being a burden to teachers. Restorative and relational pedagogy supports students holistically, allowing them to develop the necessary academic and social emotional skills needed to succeed in school and in life, skills that may be readily employed if or when a behavioral problem occurs.

THE TIME FOR CHANGE IS NOW

In January 2013, the Obama administration sponsored a "Supportive School Discipline Initiative" between the Departments of Justice and Education where the disproportionate disciplining of primarily African American males caused by zero tolerance policies was declared to be one of the most pressing civil rights issues of this decade (Shah, 2013). As a result, in January 2014, the Department of Education (DOE) issued new federal guidelines to help school leaders draft and implement school discipline policies that do not discriminate against racial or ethnic groups (U.S. Department of Education, 2014).

Under these new guidelines, the DOE Office of Civil Rights (OCR) can sanction school districts if they are found to be in violation of Title IV or VI of the Civil Rights Act of 1964. The guidelines make it clear that policies that unfairly target or affect certain groups in word or application can be considered discriminatory. Such policies are now subject to scrutiny by the OCR and schools and districts not actively working to change their policies can be sanctioned.

The resources available to schools on the DOE website are meant to help administrators become familiar with alternative discipline policies as well as to understand what kind of policies and practices could be determined as discriminatory. The guidelines provide assistance to school leaders by encouraging them to focus on creating positive environments that prevent behavioral incidents and to revise their disciplinary policies to include alternatives for addressing challenging behaviors, including restorative justice (U.S. Department of Education, 2014).

Given this exciting initiative, the time is now for school leaders to embrace educational research that consistently supports creating positive, trusting, and caring school communities that improve students' attachment to their schools and, more often than not, leads to improvements in student behavior and achievement (Bryk & Schneider, 2003; Bryk, Sebring, Allensworth, Luppescu, & Easton, 2010; Hemmings, 2012; Nor & Roslan, 2009; Riestenberg, 2012).

In addition, research clearly illustrates that principals who demonstrate a deep moral purpose and create and cultivate trusting relationships based on personal connections are most successful at implementing schoolwide reforms, including RJE (Bryk et al., 2010; Fullan, 2006a, 2008; Hemmings, 2012; Stinchcomb, Bazemore, & Riestenberg, 2006; Sumner, Silverman, & Frampton, 2010; Wadhwa, 2013; Wearmouth, McKinney, & Glynn, 2007; Youth Justice Board for England and Wales, 2004). In the following section, we introduce change theory as the theoretical framework that supports RJE as a whole school reform and discuss the role of leaders in creating and sustaining a school culture that supports change efforts.

CHANGE THEORY, LEADERSHIP, AND EMPOWERMENT

Whole school reform models intend "to provide proven schoolwide innovations that would be adopted by schools in order to improve student achievement, especially among more disadvantaged and low performing schools" (Fullan, 2008, p. 117). Theories of change identify the strategies and principles used in education reform by outlining who is involved, the role of all stakeholders needed to successfully implement change, as well as the means for measuring the effectiveness of the change at different levels (Center for Theory of Change, Inc., 2013; Fullan, 2008).

Within school contexts, change theories emphasize the role of principals in implementing successful whole school reform and encourage shared leadership among the members of the organization (Fullan, 2006a, 2006b; Hall & Hord, 2011; Hemmings, 2012; Levine & Lezotte, 1995; Morrison, 2007). The principal standing alone cannot effect change; she or he needs a committed staff supported by parents, students, and community members working to enact change together. Such successful professional relationships are built upon the four characteristics of relational trust: mutual respect, competence, personal regard, and integrity (Bryk & Schneider, 2003; Hemmings, 2012). Without the social energy created by strong relational trust, the values behind the behaviors that produce a positive school culture will break down (Bryk et al., 2010).

In table 3.2, we summarize key premises of various change theories derived from the works of leading school reformers. This table illustrates how implementing schoolwide restorative justice is a complicated and multifaceted process that requires leadership, time, collaboration, empowerment, shared values, training, and ongoing effort. In the left column, the premises of change are grouped by theme; the corresponding right column provides examples of how these premises are brought to life through actions taken in the school.

As previously stated, implementing a whole school reform such as RJE cannot be left solely to the school leader. Table 3.2 shows the connections between leaders and teachers, staff, and students who become empowered to make decisions and participate in the implementation process. In fact, many times RJE has been introduced after a teacher or student has had the opportunity to participate in training, circle, or other restorative process and then brought restorative justice back to their school (Wadhwa, 2013).

Hopkins (2011) encourages leaders who wish to implement restorative justice in their schools to let go of traditional notions of authority and instead create schools where staff and students are empowered and invited into the decision-making process. It cannot be left unsaid, however, that the concept of power sharing is threatening to many leaders and teachers; yet to counteract the negative impacts of zero tolerance policies and the current overreliance on repressive and authoritarian methods of obtaining compliance (Raible & Irizarry, 2010), administrators need to change the way they relate to staff, parents, and community as much as teachers need to change the ways they think, act, and relate to their students.

Table 3.2 Premises of Change Theory and Corresponding Examples

Premise	Examples
Motivation Moral purpose Relational trust Emotional engagement	• Visionary leadership and development of teachers-leaders/core teams • Peer support • Relationship and trust building • High expectations • High degree of relational trust
Capacity building with a focus on results Change as a team effort	• How the use of SWRAs becomes more refined over time • How leaders and teachers develop new capacities • How leader and teacher turnover affects implementation • How levels of trust between various groups in the school affects change
Learning in context Influence of context on process of change A bias for reflective action	• Includes identifying how leaders, teachers, and students learn restorative approaches right where they are • How the school climate changes as a result of this learning • Evaluating progress input and feedback from various stakeholders • Making adjustments and meeting needs
Persistence and flexibility in staying the course	• What is done to keep staff motivated and focused over time • Ongoing training and support • Training new leaders and teachers • Decreasing leader and teacher turnover

Note: Adapted from Bryk et al. (2010), Bryk and Schneider (2003), Fullan (2006b), Hall and Hord (2011), Levine and Lezotte (1995), and Morrison (2007).

This is not as simple as it sounds, even when teachers and administrators initially buy in to restorative values and processes. Institutional structures and participants have a tendency to co-opt RJ principles to reinforce a rule-based culture (Vaandering, 2013). In her qualitative study, Vaandering found that well-intentioned adults who were unacquainted and inexperienced with environments where power is shared tended to employ restorative practices to shape student behavior, thus allowing the adults to maintain their hierarchical position. Therefore, although this chapter aims to introduce RJE to school leaders, we continue to emphasize that implementing schoolwide restorative justice requires the efforts of many people and that these people need to be empowered to create and sustain change.

Characteristics of Effective School Leaders. Change theory expands upon literature regarding effective school leaders (Hemmings, 2012; Hoppey & McLeskey, 2013; May et al., 2012; Nor & Roslan, 2009; Sammons, Gu, Day, & Ko, 2011; Suber, 2011) by incorporating the role of other stakeholders essential for implementing whole school reform. We remind leaders that

RJE has the potential to be transformational (Vaandering, 2013) and therefore requires the kind of leader capable of transforming a school.

The culture of a school, although changeable, is often created over time and tends to become embedded if not entrenched. All principals must take time to learn the culture of a school, as they are ultimately responsible for creating or strengthening a productive school culture (Suber, 2011). While school climate surveys can provide important information, we believe the best way to learn the culture of any school is to listen to and observe the people in the school community. After a leader assesses the culture of a school, he or she must decide if the school is ready to change and then determine how to change it.

Consistent with change theories, RJE offers a systematic approach for changing the culture of a school. However, people in a school must be ready to embrace change; it is the leader's job to bring stakeholders together to generate excitement for change. Bryk et al. (2010) explain how relational trust reduces the risk associated with change; when people feel safe and are able to communicate honestly with each other as they build capacity, they will reach out, launch initiatives, and see them through.

If people in schools do not trust their leaders, the leader is unlikely to succeed in implementing any reform. Therefore, we strongly recommend that school leaders first reflect upon their own ability to foster trust among staff, students, and community before assessing their school's readiness for change. If relational trust is high, and a school principal is adept at empowering others, receiving input, and building a highly motivated team, the likelihood of implementing RJE with integrity and achieving positive results is high (Bryk et al., 2010; Fullan, 2006a, 2006b).

Several studies emphasize that schools need clear information about what RJ is and what it is not, how it will be implemented, and by whom (Sumner et al., 2010; Youth Justice Board for England and Wales, 2004). Before starting any initiative, principals, staff, and teachers need assurance that the necessary resources, including initial and ongoing training, in-service workshops where teachers can build capacity by sharing success stories, and integration into the behavior policy will be available over the long term (Reimer, 2011; Sumner et al., 2010). In the following section, we provide some suggestions for how school leaders who wish to change their school's culture through schoolwide restorative justice can learn more and begin.

WHERE TO START

There is no set way to implement RJE, just as there are many points of entry into the school. Here, we provide practical ways for principals to learn more about RJE and its implementation, based on both conversations with a myriad of practitioners working every day in schools and research on RJE. First, we strongly recommend that leaders resist the urge to do something quickly and expect immediate results; as in all whole school reform efforts, the degree to which initiatives are implemented with integrity greatly affects the outcomes (Fullan, 2008). Instead, we encourage a more intentional, long-term implementation of restorative justice and ask leaders to consider the following suggestions.

Learn All That You Can Before You Begin. Before embarking on any new initiative, it is important that school leaders know where they are now and where they want to go. Everyone, not just school leaders, needs to know enough about RJE to determine if it is a good fit for their school. It is important, then, that teachers, coaches, counselors, and other key personnel are sufficiently knowledgeable about restorative justice so that they can more effectively facilitate its implementation. This core team should consist of those most excited about adopting RJE and most willing to put in the extra effort to make it happen, as they will motivate others to embrace restorative justice over time (Fullan, 2006a).

Additionally, becoming more knowledgeable about RJE can help to ensure that the outcome is a positive change in school culture, not simply the insertion of a new program. The former will facilitate a more positive environment; the latter will likely fail. In schools where RJE was introduced as a program, particularly one tied to grant funding, the program ended either when the grant funding ended or when resources were diverted to another program (Reimer, 2011; Wadhwa, 2013).

An excellent resource for learning more about the implementation of RJE is the Minnesota Department of Education. Minnesota began practicing RJE in 1998 and now promotes restorative justice in all schools. The MN DOE has a wealth of information readily available on its website.

We recommend reading both the theory of RJE and the anecdotal and empirical research related to its implementation. Schools that have implemented RJE in their schools and conducted systematic research or program evaluation on such implementation have provided valuable insight regarding lessons learned along the way. Reimer (2011) administered questionnaires and conducted interviews with teachers in a school that had implemented RJ and found, among other things, that teachers were more comfortable implementing RJ in their classrooms when their school community exemplified the values of restorative justice.

This finding highlights the importance of working to create a more restorative school culture and not simply implementing restorative justice only as a means of addressing challenging behaviors. In addition, a deeper understanding of the theoretical foundations of restorative justice in education will provide a solid rationale for implementing RJE as a whole school reform and will highlight the cultural transformation it aims to create.

Talking with others who have implemented or are in the process of implementing restorative approaches in their schools is most advantageous. Restorative justice programs have been implemented in schools in many districts across the country, including Baltimore, San Francisco, Oakland, Denver, Los Angeles, Minneapolis, Philadelphia, and Milwaukee, to name just a few. Fairfax, Virginia's Restorative Justice Initiative, is currently being implemented in over two hundred schools.

We recommend connecting with other leaders involved in restorative approaches by attending conferences and trainings related to RJE. Organizations such as the National Association for Community and Restorative Justice, the International Institute for Restorative Practices (IIRP), and Conflict Resolution in Education hold regularly scheduled conferences that bring together people who are implementing restorative justice in their schools and provide excellent avenues for both learning and networking.

Build a Shared Vision among Faculty and Staff. RJE is most effectively implemented after leaders first gain support from faculty and staff. When restorative justice (or any other initiative, for that matter) is mandated by administrators without input from teachers, it is met with opposition which then jeopardizes effective implementation (Fullan, 2006a; Reimer, 2011; Wadhwa, 2013). In order to garner such support and promote faculty buy-in, we recommend having open conversations with faculty about shared goals for the school and ways in which restorative justice might meet those shared goals.

Change theories encourage principals to develop leaders throughout the school who will provide input and feedback as well as motivation for continued training and implementation (Fullan, 2006a; Hall & Hord, 2011; Levine & Lezotte, 1995). For example, if teachers express that school safety is a priority for them, help them make connections between school safety and healthy relationships that restorative approaches and relational pedagogies facilitate.

In one school, teachers were concerned about high truancy rates; after agreeing that this was a priority they wanted to address, the principal formed a team of teachers and school faculty who investigated ways in which truancy had been addressed in other schools. By reading and consulting with a local restorative justice circle facilitator, the team found that greater connections to the school community had been shown to increase student attendance. The team went on to share with the rest of the school the ways in which restorative approaches could impact students' sense of school connectedness, promoting buy-in among faculty and better attendance rates among students (Blood & Thorsborne, 2005; Gregory, Skiba, & Noguera, 2010).

It is often helpful to find a group of teachers who are already exemplifying one or more of the restorative values and experiencing positive outcomes. By bringing attention to their effectiveness, and working to make what they are doing more explicitly linked to restorative justice approaches, effective teachers become mentors and models for their colleagues. When teachers are given space and invited to talk together about how they incorporate restorative values and pedagogies into their classroom instruction, professional learning communities emerge organically and capacity building occurs naturally as teachers and others gain experience and become more empowered (Fullan, 2006a; Hopkins, 2004).

Look for Ways to Make Small Changes at First. There are a number of things that can be done at first without a full-scale overhaul of the school. Many schools have some type of in-school suspension (ISS) program that keeps students in school while still separating them for a time from their peers. Often, these programs are designed in ways that are primarily punitive in nature, leaving students to face consequences without actually learning anything from the consequences.

Small changes to the design of the ISS program can change its intent from punitive to restorative. By providing a space for students to participate in restorative conferencing related to their behavior and ensuring that students in ISS are treated with dignity and respect, schools can help students use the time in ISS to better understand the affects their behavior has on others and on their own academic success (Evans, 2013).

These small changes that build on what is already working well within the school lay the groundwork for adopting restorative justice more widely across all school environments. If elementary teachers are already having carpet circle times in the morning, consider using that time with young children to initiate community-building circles using a talking piece as a way to help them get in touch with their own emotions and to learn perspective taking, empathy, and active listening skills (CASEL, n.d.; Pranis, 2005, 2007).

If a high school already has an advisory program in place, consider ways to use that designated time to intentionally focus on addressing conflict resolution strategies, increasing the opportunities for students and faculty to develop SEL competencies, or holding circle processes for building healthy relationships between students and teachers. These small changes can go a long way in changing the overall climate of the school, will promote healthy relationships that prevent unwanted behaviors, and will facilitate addressing challenging behaviors when they happen.

Replace Punitive Discipline Procedures with Polices That Promote Restorative Practices. We are proposing RJE as a whole school reform that improves school climate in light of sufficient evidence that exclusionary discipline (i.e., suspensions and expulsions) serves to erode, not enhance, school safety (American Psychological Association, 2008; Kupchik, 2010; Simon,

2007; Skiba & Peterson, 2000). Thus, we recommend adopting discipline and other policies that promote safety and community between and among students and faculty, which keep students in school, and that work with challenging students to address their behavior rather than removing them.

For example, a student who is chronically tardy will benefit more from some supportive mentoring in organization, self-responsibility, and time management than they would from being suspended for three days. Some students who demonstrate disrespectful behaviors may be expressing a belief that school is irrelevant and academically frustrating or that they feel disrespected themselves. Suspending them for those behaviors might serve to reinforce their beliefs and subsequently exacerbate undesired behaviors, while restorative conferences with teachers and students lead to increased understanding about students' needs and an opportunity to build student investment in school (Wearmouth et al., 2007). Changing school discipline policies to reflect restorative values promotes a growth model for discipline rather than simply a punitive model.

Replacing zero tolerance policies with policies that promote restorative practices will facilitate more effective, relationally based discipline. In that, restorative justice assumes that students' behavior is actually a type of communication (Evans & Lester, 2012), restorative practitioners attend to students' behavior to find out what is provoking conflict, disengagement, or resistance. Thus, even when consequences are given for inappropriate behaviors, those consequences should be accompanied by an opportunity to be heard and to learn new behaviors in a supportive environment. Further, when possible, having policies in place that include students' input in decisions about the types of consequences they face promotes self-regulation and problem-solving skills, dispositions that will help them beyond the immediate situation and promote more prosocial behavior in the future (CASEL, n.d.; Day-Vines & Terriquez, 2008).

In one school, three fifth graders destroyed a fence that ran between the school and the neighbor's yard. The principal met with the boys and asked them what they might do to fix the fence. After deliberating for a day, and with some guidance from one of their teachers, the boys developed a plan to raise money for purchasing the necessary materials. Using their lunch period each day to work on the fence under the voluntary supervision of one of the school's maintenance workers, the boys repaired the damage. The boys later reported that being encouraged to resolve the situation on their own resulted in their being more aware of the consequences of their actions. They also appreciated the adults who cared enough to invest time in the process, in addition to learning how to build a fence.

Restorative approaches also hold significant benefit to those impacted by such behavior. Within punitive discipline systems, students who experience harm by the behaviors of other students very rarely have their own needs met in those situations and in many cases, policies prevent processes that might address their needs. On the contrary, a principal in one school who was committed to restorative approaches responded to complaints by some Muslim students about harassment by creating a weekly circle time for those students to meet and share their experiences and receive support by an adult trained in restorative circle facilitation. Thus, in addition to having policies in place that dealt with bullying, this principal enacted a process that addressed the impact of bullying on the Muslim students. Initiating policies and practices that meet the needs of students being impacted by harmful behavior works to promote a more restorative school culture.

Model Restorative and Relational Pedagogies. At its core, restorative justice is not simply a program to be implemented but rather a way of seeing and a way of being (Pranis, 2007); as such, it is guided by the types of values and principles that have been discussed in this chapter. If culture change is to happen in schools, it has to start with the leadership. This means that principals and other administrators and leaders must, first and foremost, begin acting in ways that are consistent with the values and principles of restorative and relational pedagogy (Vaandering, 2013).

One of the core principles of restorative justice is an emphasis on respect and the development of a school culture where all students—regardless of their ability, their race or ethnicity, their gender or sexual orientation, sexual identity, or any other area of difference—are valued and treated with dignity.

School leaders play a significant role in setting the tone for this type of culture by first treating faculty and staff, regardless of their differences, with respect and dignity. In a political climate where teachers are often disrespected and devalued based on the results of standardized assessments, many teachers experience demoralization and frustration; as a result, many good teachers are leaving the profession. Administrators can increase their support and express value for teachers, modeling the types of relationships that they hope to see in their schools.

Further, administrators can impact the school climate by asking restorative questions and practicing active listening, particularly when conflict arises. Ueland (1998) suggested that before we can learn to listen, we first need to feel that we have been heard. By exemplifying restorative values in the mid of tense situations, the principles of restorative justice become more than theories; teachers and staff who experience restorative processes first-hand are more likely to enact those principles and practices in their own classrooms (Vaandering, 2013). Principals have the unique opportunity to facilitate these types of relational climates by modeling the types of dispositions and behaviors that lead to more restorative school cultures.

CONCLUSION

In conclusion, we acknowledge that in order to radically alter the trajectory of school discipline by creating safe, positive, and caring school environments, there is a need for both education policy and school culture change. Systemic, top-down mandates are often a necessary part of beginning new initiatives (Hall & Hord, 2011); however, there must also be buy-in from faculty and staff and a change in attitudes, beliefs, and practices for these initiatives to be sustainable (Fullan, 2008).

School leaders, including teacher mentors, principals, academic coaches, and guidance counselors, hold a great deal of influence in the type of culture that is established in schools. This chapter has provided a general understanding of restorative justice in education. Additionally, it has served to support school leaders in their quest to create better schools where children feel safe and can focus on academic learning, while at the same time learning the social and emotional skills they need to succeed in life.

REFERENCES

American Psychological Association. (2008). Are zero tolerance policies effective in the schools? An evidentiary review and recommendations. *American Psychologist*, *63*(9), 852–862. doi:10.1037/0003066X.63.9.852

Blood, P., & Thorsborne, M. (2005, March). The challenge of culture change: Embedding restorative practice in schools. Paper presented at the Sixth International Conference on Conferencing, Circles and other Restorative practices. Sydney, Australia.

Brown, T. M. (2007). Lost and turned out: Academic, social and emotional experiences of students excluded from school. *Urban Education*, *42*(5), 432–455.

Browne-Dianis, J. (2011). Stepping back from zero tolerance. *Educational Leadership*, (1), 24–28.

Bryk, A. S., & Schneider, B. (2003). Trust in schools: A core resource for school reform. *Educational Leadership*, *60*(6), 40–44.

Bryk, A. S., Sebring, P. B., Allensworth, E., Luppescu, S., & Easton, J. Q. (2010). *Organizing schools for improvement: Lessons from Chicago.* Chicago, IL: The University of Chicago Press.

Cassella, R. (2003). Zero tolerance policy in schools: Rationale, consequences and alternatives. *Teachers College Record*, *105*(5), 872–892.

Center for Theory of Change, Inc. (2013). *What is theory of change?* Retrieved from https://www.theoryofchange.org

Claassen, R., & Claassen, R. (2008). *Discipline that restores.* South Carolina: BookSurge.

Collaborative for Academic and Social Emotional Learning (CASEL). (n.d.). *Social and emotional learning core competencies.* Retrieved from http://www.casel.org/social-and-emotional-learning/core-competencies

Davis, A. (2012). *The meaning of freedom and other difficult dialogues.* San Francisco, CA: City Lights Books.

Day-Vines, N. L., & Terriquez, V. (2008). A strengths-based approach to promoting prosocial behavior among African American and Latino students. *Professional School Counseling, 12*(2), 170–175.

Dohrn, B. (2001). Look out kid/It's something you did. In W. Ayers, B. Dohrn, & R. Ayers (Eds.), *Zero tolerance: Resisting the drive for punishment in our schools* (pp. 89–113). New York, NY: The New Press.

Evans, K. R. (2013). Doing time in ISS: A performance of school discipline. In R. Gabriel & J. N. Lester (Eds.), *Performances of research: Critical issues in K-12 education.* New York, NY: Peter Lang.

Evans, K. R., & Lester, J. N. (2012). Zero tolerance: Moving the conversation forward. *Intervention in School and Clinic, 48*(2), 108–114.

Evans, K. R., & Lester, J. N. (2013). Restorative justice in education: What we know so far. *Middle School Journal, 44*(5), 57–63.

Fullan, M. (2006a). Change theory: A force for school improvement. Seminar Series Paper No. 157, November, 2006. Victoria, BC: Center for Strategic Education. Retrieved from http://www.michaelfullan.com/media/13396072630.pdf

Fullan, M. (2006b). The future of educational change: System thinkers in action. *Journal of Educational Change, 7,* 113–122. doi:10.1007/s10833-006-9003-9

Fullan, M. (2008). Curriculum implementation and sustainability. In F. M. Connelly (Ed.), *The Sage handbook of curriculum and instruction* (pp. 113–122). Thousand Oaks, CA: Sage.

Gillborn, D. (2010). Reform, racism and the centrality of whiteness: Assessment, ability and the "new eugenics." *Irish Educational Studies, 29*(3), 231–252.

Goleman, D. (1995). *Emotional intelligence: Why it can matter more than IQ.* New York, NY: Bantam Books.

Gonzalez, T. (2012). Keeping kids in schools: Restorative justice, punitive discipline, and the school to prison pipeline. *Journal of Law & Education, 41*(2), 281–335.

Gregory, A., Skiba, R. J., & Noguera, P. A. (2010). The achievement gap and the discipline gap: Two sides of the same coin? *Educational Researcher, 39*(1), 59–68.

Hall, G. E., & Hord, S. M. (2011). *Implementing change: Patterns, principles, and potholes* (3rd ed.). Upper Saddle River, NJ: Pearson Education.

Hemmings, A. (2012). Four Rs for urban high school reform: Re-envisioning, reculturation, restructuring, and remoralization. *Improving Schools, 15*(3), 198–210. doi:10.1177/1365480212458861

Hirschfield, P. J. (2008). Preparing for prison? The criminalization of school discipline in the USA. *Theoretical Criminology, 12*(1), 79–101. doi:10.1177/1362480607085795

Hoffman, S. (2014). Zero benefit: Estimating the effect of zero tolerance discipline polices on racial disparities in school discipline. *Educational Policy, 28*(1), 69–95. doi:10.1177/0895904812453999

Hopkins, B. (2004). *Just schools: A whole school approach to restorative justice.* London, England: Jessica Kingsley.

Hopkins, B. (2011). *The restorative classroom: Using restorative approaches to foster effective learning.* London, England: Optimus Education.

Hoppey, D., & McLeskey, J. (2013). A case study of principal leadership in an effective inclusive school. *Journal of Special Education, 46*(4), 245–256. doi:10.1177/0022466910390507

Hulac, D., Terrell, J., Vining, O., & Berstein, J. (2011). *Behavioral interventions in schools: A response-to-intervention guidebook.* New York, NY: Routledge.

Jones, K. (2013). #zerotolerance #KeepingupwiththeTimes: How federal zero tolerance policies failed to promote educational success, deter juvenile legal consequences, and confront new social media concerns in public schools. *Journal of Law & Education, 42*(4), 739–749.

Karp, D. R., & Breslin, B. (2001). Restorative justice in school communities. *Youth & Society, 33*(2), 249–272.

Kennedy-Lewis, B. (2013). Using critical policy analysis to examine competing discourses in zero tolerance legislation: Do we really want to leave no child behind? *Journal of Education Policy, 29*(2), 165–194.

Kliebard, H. M. (2009). The rise of scientific curriculum-making and its aftermath. In D. J. Flinders & S. J. Thornton (Eds.), *The curriculum studies reader* (3rd ed., pp. 52–61). New York, NY: Routledge.

Kupchik, A. (2010). Homeroom security: School discipline in an age of fear. New York: New York University Press.

Ladson-Billings, G. (2001). America still eats her young. In W. Ayers, B. Dohrn, & R. Ayers (Eds.), *Zero tolerance: Resisting the drive for punishment in our schools* (pp. 77–85). New York, NY: The New Press.

Levine, D. U., & Lezotte, L. W. (1995). Effective schools research. In J. A. Banks & C. A. McGee Banks (Eds.), *Handbook of research on multicultural education* (pp. 525–545). New York, NY: Macmillan Pub.

Macready, T. (2009). Learning social responsibility in schools: A restorative practice. *Educational Psychology in Practice, 25*(3), 211–220.

May, H., Huff, J., & Goldring, E. (2012). A longitudinal study of principals' activities and student performance. *School Effectiveness and School Improvement, 23*(4), 417–439. doi:10.1080/09243453.2012.678866

Moore, M. (2011). Psychological theories of crime and delinquency. *Journal of Human Behavior in the Social Environment, 21*(3), 226–239. doi:10.1080/10911359.2011.564552

Morrison, B. (2006). School bullying and restorative justice: Toward a theoretical understanding of the role of respect, pride, and shame. *Journal of Social Issues, 62*(2), 371–392.

Morrison, B. (2007). *Restoring safe school communities: A whole school response to bullying, violence and alienation.* Sydney, Australia: The Federation Press.

Morrison, B. E., & Vaandering, D. (2012). Restorative justice: Pedagogy, praxis, and discipline. *Journal of School Violence, 11*(2), 138–155.

Nguyen, N. (2013). Scripting "safe" schools: Mapping urban education and zero tolerance during the long war. *Review of Education, Pedagogy & Cultural Studies, 35*(4), 277–297. doi:10.1080/10714413.2013.819725

Nor, S. M., & Roslan, S. (2009). Turning around at-risk schools: What effective principals do. *International Journal on School Disaffection, 6*(2), 21–29.

Pranis, K. (2005). *The little book of circle processes: A new/old approach to peace-making.* Intercourse, PA: Good Books.

Pranis, K. (2007). Restorative values. In G. Johnstone & D. W. Van Ness (Eds.), *Handbook of restorative justice* (pp. 59–74). Cullompton, Devon: Willan.

Raible, J., & Irizarry, J. G. (2010). Redirecting the teacher's gaze: Teacher education, youth surveillance and the school-to-prison pipeline. *Teaching and Teacher Education, 26*(5), 1196–1203.

Reimer, K. (2011). An exploration of the implementation of restorative justice in an Ontario public school. *Canadian Journal of Educational Administration and Policy,* (119). Retrieved from http://www.umanitoba.ca/publications/cjeap/pdf_files/reimer.pdf

Reyes, A. H. (2006). *Discipline, achievement, race.* Lanham, MD: Rowman & Littlefield Education.

Riestenberg, N. (2012). *Circle in the square: Building community and repairing harm in school.* St. Paul, MN: Living Justice Press.

Rodriquez, L. F. (2013). Moving beyond test-prep pedagogy: Dialoguing with multicultural preservice teachers for a quality education. *Multicultural Education, 15*(3), 133–140. doi:10.1080/15210960.2013.809302

Sammons, P., Gu, Q., Day, C., & Ko, J. (2011). Exploring the impact of school leadership on pupil outcomes: Results from a study of academically improved and effective schools in England. *International Journal of Educational Management, 25*(1), 83–101.

Sellman, E., Cremin, H., & McCluskey, G. (2013). *Restorative approaches to conflict in schools: Interdisciplinary perspectives on whole school approaches to managing relationships.* Abingdon, OX: Routledge.

Shah, N. (2013, April 8). New analysis bolsters case against suspension, researchers say. *Education Week.* Retrieved from http://www.edweek.org/ew/index.html

Simon, J. (2007). *Governing through crime: How the war on crime transformed American democracy and created a culture of fear.* London, England: Oxford University Press.

Skiba, R. (2001). When is disproportionality discrimination? The overrepresentation of Black students in school suspension. In W. Ayers, B. Dohrn, & R. Ayers (Eds.), *Zero tolerance: Resisting the drive for punishment in our schools* (pp. 176–187). New York, NY: The New Press.

Skiba, R. J., & Peterson, R. L. (2000). School discipline at a crossroads: From zero tolerance to early response. *Exceptional Children, 66*(3), 335–347.

Skiba, R. J., Arrendondo, M. I., & Rausch, M. K. (2014). *New and developing research on disparities in discipline.* Bloomington, IN: The Equity Project, Center for Evaluation and Education Policy.

Stinchcomb, J. B., Bazemore, G., & Riestenberg, N. (2006). Beyond zero tolerance: Restoring justice in secondary schools. *Youth Violence and Juvenile Justice, 4*(2), 123–147.

Stutzman Amstutz, L., & Mullet, J. H. (2005). *The little book of restorative discipline for schools.* Intercourse, PA: Good Books.

Suber, C. (2011). Characteristics of effective principals in high-poverty South Carolina elementary schools. Retrieved from http://cnx.org/content/m41761/1.1/

Sumner, M. D., Silverman, C. J., & Frampton, M. L. (2010). School-based restorative justice as an alternative to zero-tolerance policies: Lessons from West Oakland. Report by Thelton E. *Henderson Center for Social Justice.* Berkeley, CA. Retrieved from http://www.law.berkeley.edu/files/11-2010_School-based_ Restorative_Justice_As_an_Alternative_to_Zero-Tolerance_Policies.pdf

Teske, S. C. (2011). A study of zero tolerance policies in schools: A multi-integrated systems approach to improve outcomes for adolescents. *Journal of Child & Adolescent Psychiatric Nursing, 24*(2), 88–97. doi:10.1111/j.1744-6171.2011.00273.x

Ueland, B. (1998). *Tell me more: On the fine art of listening.* Tucson, AZ: Kore Press.

U.S. Department of Education. (2014). *U.S. Departments of Education and Justice release school discipline guidance package to enhance school climate and improve school discipline policies/practices.* Retrieved from http://www.ed.gov/news/press- releases/ us-departments-education-and-justice-release-school-discipline-guidance-package-

Vaandering, D. (2010). The significance of critical theory for restorative justice in education. *Review of Education, Pedagogy, and Cultural Studies, 32*(2), 145–176. doi:10.1080/10714411003799165

Vaandering, D. D. (2013). Student, teacher, and administrator perspectives on harm: Implications for implementing safe and caring school initiatives. *Review of Education, Pedagogy & Cultural Studies, 35*(4), 298–318. doi:10.1080/10714413.2013.825514

Wadhwa, A. (2013). *Race, discipline, and critical restorative justice in two urban high schools.* Unpublished doctoral dissertation. Harvard University, Boston, MA.

Wearmouth, J., McKinney, R., & Glynn, T. (2007). Restorative justice: Two examples from the New Zealand schools. *British Journal of Special Education, 34,* 196–203.

Youth Justice Board for England and Wales. (2004). *National evaluation of the restorative justice in schools programme.* Retrieved from http://dera.ioe.ac.uk/ 5926/1/nat%20ev%20of%20rj%20in%20schoolsfullfv.pdf

Zehr, H. (2002). *The little book of restorative justice.* Intercourse, PA: Good Books.

Zembroski, D. (2011). Sociological theories of crime and delinquency. *Journal of Human Behavior in the Social Environment, 21*(3), 240–254. doi:10.1080/ 10911359.2011.564553

Chapter Four

White High School Administrators as Racial Advisors

Bryan Davis

INTRODUCTION

As high school student populations become more racially diverse, the racial makeup of high school administrators continues to be overwhelmingly white. White high school administrators leading more racially diverse student bodies face an increased number of racial encounters in high schools. This chapter examines how white high school administrators take on the role of what the researcher describes as "racial advisor," explore the complexity of such a role, and consider how transformative leadership theory can offer a basis for dialogue and action to generate hope toward an improved educational experience for all of students.

For school administrators, the role of racial advisor is not assigned, defined, or even desired. However, racial advising is an integral part of the administrator's role. The question is not whether or not an administrator should be a racial advisor. They *are* racial advisors, advising on racial situations at the frantic pace of a school day. Most school administrators are not prepared to take on a role of racial advisor. In fact, the role is unexamined in school leadership research and unexplored in educational administration preparation coursework.

The white high school administrators described in this chapter, like many of their peers, have not grown up in racially diverse environments where they have experienced the direct impact of race. These white high school administrators, in their roles as racial advisors, are left to engage in situations involving race without a complete perspective of the impact of race on their own lives and the lives of the students and families of color they serve.

We will define the role of racial advisor for white high school administrators through the use of empirical evidence and provide practical recommendations of how to improve preparation for this role through transformative leadership theory. Acknowledging the role of high school administrators as racial advisors and providing insight into how to become effective racial advisors will move our high schools forward in becoming more inclusive learning environments.

OVERVIEW OF THE PROJECT

This chapter is written with data collected from a dissertation, which explored perspectives on how white high school administrators make meaning of whiteness (Davis, 2011). The study provided space for white high school administrators, who rarely had thought about the implications of their race in relationship to their role as school leaders. McIntyre (1997) sees this type of reflection as necessary in order to address racism in schools. The lack of self-reflection about being a white person in this society distances white people from investigating the meaning of whiteness and prohibits a critical examination of the individual, institutional, and cultural forms of racism.

For white educators, in particular, this invisibility to one's own racial being has implications in one's teaching practice—which includes such things as the choice of curriculum materials, student expectations, grading procedures, and assessment techniques—just to name a few. What is necessary for white teachers is an opportunity to problematize race in such a way that it breaks open the dialogue about white privilege, white advantage, and the white ways of thinking and knowing that dominate education in the United States.

McIntyre's assertions also apply to white high school administrators. School administrators enforce student discipline, supervise teachers, and assist in the creation of school policy. In doing so, school administrators create the culture of learning for their schools and they are powerful people in leadership positions who are capable of maintaining the status quo or moving a school toward improved learning for students of all races.

This study used a qualitative research method drawing from case study and autoethnography as the methodology. The case study data was comprised of ten individual interviews and three focus groups with five white high school administrators from a large high school in the Midwest. Data collection for the autoethnography included the researcher's field notes and a personal journal.

Critical White Studies provided the theoretical context for the researcher's interpretation and theorization of how administrators made meaning of their whiteness (Perry, 2001). Critical White Studies focuses on whiteness in order to better understand and disrupt its predominance. The process of focusing on whiteness involves an effort to get beyond received wisdoms and ask basic questions about race, power, and society. Allen (1999) writes:

The fight against Whiteness means that White people need to intervene in the process which produced their privileged White identity. Critical studies of Whiteness argue that what oppressed people of color need from White people is not sympathy as much as a self and collective-reflection on their own White privilege in a system of White racism. (p. 3)

Critical White Studies is rooted in Critical Race Theory and DeCuir and Dixon (2004) describe Critical Race Theory using five tenets: Counter Storytelling, Permanence of Racism, and Whiteness as Property, Interest Convergence, and Critique of Liberalism. Counter storytelling is telling stories that give "voice to marginalized groups" and "[h]elp us to understand what life is like for others" (DeCuir & Dixon, 2004).

An example of counter storytelling is African American students providing perspective to white school administrators on their experiences in school. Permanence of racism is accepting that racism is a permanent part of American life. The permanence of racism is also realizing racism as a conscious and unconscious act that privileges white people. This critique is effective when countering ideas of solving a racial problem in our society.

The idea is that racism may be gone from that situation but will prove permanent by reappearing in another context as racism. Whiteness as property deploys whiteness as a property right and incorporates "policies and practices" that reinforce white privilege (DeCuir & Dixon, 2004). An example of using whiteness as property is a school referring an overrepresented number of students of color for special education. The referral to special education results in lower academic expectations and lower achievement.

Interest convergence offers concessions that do not disrupt the "normal way of life for White people" (DeCuir & Dixon, 2004). An example of interest convergence is a school wanting a student of color to attend for because of their athletic ability, whereas the student may have academic reasons for enrolling. The academic expectations from the school may be lower for this student than what is expected from other students, creating a gap of expectations between the student and the school.

Critique of liberalism argues the notion of colorblindness, neutrality of the law, and incremental change. An example would be a white school administrator who believes that race does not matter, which may result in students not having an opportunity to develop their racial identity in a meaningful way. Based on the scholarship of Critical White Studies, five tenets provide an outline for studying white school administrators as racial advisors. Critical Race Theory is indeed informative when applied to the context of school administration.

However, there is another concept that draws from Critical White Studies that contends whiteness is invisible. Perry (2001) and Frankenberg (1993) have articulated a widespread understanding that white culture is "invisible" because it is constructed as "normal." As the norm, white culture has no definition, only those who deviate from the norm have "culture" and therein lays the toxicity of the construction of white as the (cultureless) norm. Whiteness then serves as a basis on which to measure the humanity and social standing of others. Anything different from the normed white culture is considered different and typically inferior. Grover (1996) writes:

> White is transparent. That's the point of being the dominant race. Sure, the Whiteness is there, but you never think of it. If you're White, you never have to think of it. Sometimes when folks make a point of thinking of it, some (not all) of them run the risk of being either sappy in the eyes of other White people or of being dangerous to non-White people. And if White folks remind each other about being White, too often the reminder is about threats by outsiders, - nonwhite people-, who steal entitlements like good jobs, a fine education, nice neighborhoods, and the good life. (p. 34)

This quote emphasizes the need for meaningful and respectful conversations about race. Without practice of how to engage in conversations about race, we cannot expect administrators to become insightful decision makers on racial issues in our schools.

ROLE OF RACIAL ADVISORS

During this study, the researcher noticed and became curious about the role white school administrators assumed as racial advisors in their school. White administrators were key players in defining racism in the school because of the job they are expected to do with students, families, staff, and the community. The administrators made decisions involving race during the speed of a school day, which left them with little to no time to process and reflect on their decisions involving race.

There is no way for school administrators to avoid this role. Whether or not they should be racial advisors is debatable, if there was a choice. However, in this case, there is no choice. Every school administrator, no matter his or her race, is a racial advisor. Their authority in student and staff discipline, school policy, and curriculum development and teacher supervision places them in a powerful position that requires decisions to be made on how race and racism are defined within the school.

In this research white high school principals, acting as racial advisors, defined racism through their daily practices in the privacy of their offices with individual students and in public with large amounts of people. Both types of racial interactions provide opportunities for school administrators to discuss and define race within a school setting. In the next section, we describe how a white school administrator experienced racial advising.

Racial advising many times takes place with individual interactions between the school administrator and a student or small group of students. These conversations about race are where racism in a school is defined in practice. This places the school administrator in a position to frame discourse around racism for the school.

One white administrator in this study, Meghan, described the racial advising she did with students. Meghan is a 40-year-old, white female who has been an associate principal at South Side High School for the past eight years. South Side High School is located in a Midwestern city of approximately one hundred thousand people. The school is part of a district serving approximately twenty thousand students. South Side High School enrolls 2242 students and employs 149 faculty members. In 2010, 75 percent of the student population was white and 99 percent of the teaching population was white. In 1998–1999, 89 percent of the student population was white (Davis, 2011). This racial demographic transformation allowed race to be a noticeable difference in the school over the past ten years.

Meghan grew up in Riverton, Midwest, a primarily white community, with little experience interacting with people of color. She recalls inappropriate racial comments from her family that set her standard of racism. These comments would involve her white family members using derogatory names in reference to people of color. Meghan knew that these derogatory comments were inappropriate and marked them as racist. From her perspective, anything that was not using a derogatory racist comment was not racist.

Meghan describes a situation we would define as racial advising at an individual level. She was asked: "Share a story that you remember where being White in a situation mattered. Who was involved? How did you feel? How did it impact you?" Meghan's response was:

I've never made a big issue out of race. One time I was accused of being racist. It was a Hispanic family. They accused me of being racist because I court-referred their child and I was always getting them down to the office. The family requested that they have a different Associate Principal. And so, they switched to Ruth M., because she speaks Spanish. They figured she wouldn't discriminate. And then she court-referred him and suspended him. And, things hadn't changed. But, that was the first time I had been called racist. It didn't bother me so much because I didn't feel I was. I can't recall if I did something that they thought I had discriminated against him because of his race. They never mentioned anything, but it's always in the back of my mind. And so I – I think I – I think I – I try to do okay. It sticks in my mind because I'd never been called that. I've had kids come in and complain. That teacher's being racist and here's why. And—and these kids are being racist and here's why. And—and, I have taught the kids.

And, I have—I have affirmed that yes; you know what? There are people who are racist. But, here are some examples of some racist things. And, here's some not. And, here's what you need to work through. And, here's how you should handle it and so on. (Davis, 2011, p. 99)

In essence, Meghan, from her position of authority, is defining racism in her school and advising students how to navigate racism. This is part of her role as a school administrator; she is a racial advisor. Problematic in Meghan defining racism for her school is her focus on individual actions. Her definitions are grounded in her previous experiences of derogatory racist remarks made by her white relatives. This leaves her focused on individual comments to eliminate racism leaving her oblivious to societal and institutional racism that occurs in the school. Meghan was also pressured to address racism because there was a School Board policy requiring that students not be treated differently because of their race. The School Board policy stated:

The Cityville School District shall comply with all legal requirements not to discriminate on the basis of sex, race, color, religion, national origin, ancestry, creed, pregnancy, marital or parental status, sexual orientation, gender identity, gender expression, gender non-conformity, social, socio-economic or family status, physical attributes, disability/handicap or any other basis protected by state or federal law in policies, programs and procedures. The District shall *not*, on the basis of the above listed categories:

1. Treat one person differently from another in determining whether such a person satisfies any requirement or condition for the receipt of service, aid and benefit.
2. Provide different service, aid or benefit.
3. Provide service, aid or benefit in a different manner.
4. Deny any person any such service, aid or benefit.
5. Subject any person to separate or different rules of behavior, sanction or other treatment.
6. Discriminate against any person in the application of any rules of appearance.
7. Aid or perpetuate discrimination against any person by providing significant assistance to any agency, organization or person which discriminates in providing any aid, benefit or service to students.
8. Otherwise limit any person in the enjoyment of any right, privilege, advantage or opportunity.
(Retrieved on January 17, 2011, from http://www.gbaps.org)

This policy may be intended to ensure all students are treated equally; however, by identifying differences of race between students while acting as a racial advisor, Meghan is moving toward violating school board policy. These types of policies can leave an administrator with a paralyzed sense of what to do as a racial advisor when issues of race are brought to their attention. School administrators must realize that the School Board policy is a wide boundary for the district and there can and must be many different paths to administering the policy that take into account the student experiences.

White school administrators must be prepared to be racial advisors for students of color. Unfortunately, Meghan had no previous experience analyzing the influence of race critically within a school. The lack of a critical perspective on race makes her influence as a racial advisor very dangerous. Without a perspective of their influence as racial beings, Meghan and other white administrators will not see the connections between racism on a personal and institutional level. This lack of perspective will continue to disenfranchise students and families of color who are experiencing racism at school and in the community.

While Meghan's racial advising was focused on individual interactions with students of color in her office, white school administrators also perform racial advising in interactions with white students in large group settings. As a white administrator, advising white students in racial situations creates a different dynamic. In a way, this is a more comfortable situation of race to address because the administrator is talking with people who may have similar racial experiences to themselves. However, it is also a potentially more dangerous situation because the administrator may not be forced to address the issues of racism because it has become embedded in the culture of the school and community, thus it becomes transparent. This allows the administrator with the option to not address racist actions, furthering the culture of white dominance, without needing to feel accountable or even being aware that this is happening.

Addressing large groups of students in a public setting also puts the racial advisor role in a different position than the advising for individual students. The larger group provides more support to racist actions with a collective sense of identity that includes not only the students but in some cases parents, staff members, and community members that are present at the event. The large numbers of people, in many cases primarily white, provide support for these racist actions to occur by their inaction as the actual event is occurring. Their inaction may be a result of being oblivious to the racism, confused and paralyzed of what to do to address racism or supportive of it. This places additional pressure on the school administrator as a racial advisor to act on the racist actions without knowing how the group will react to the racism being addressed.

School administrators are often in charge of supervising large groups of students at after-school activities that draw large public crowds. Football games, basketball games, and school musicals are good examples of large group events school administrators oversee in their role. An example of how racial advising may occur in a large group event occurred when the researcher assumed a principal position at a high school. The setting was a high school varsity boys' basketball game, which decided bragging rights on the West side of Cityville. The game was expected to have a high attendance in a gym that had a seating capacity of two thousand.

Cityville West Side High School is located on a Native American Reservation on the Southwest side of Cityville and enrolls one thousand four hundred students. The student population at Cityville West is 80 percent white, 10 percent Native American, and 10 percent combination of African American, Asian, and Hispanic students. Cityville North High School enrolls eleven hundred students. The student population is 60 percent white, 15 percent African American, 15 percent Native American, and 10 percent Asian.

The researcher walked into the gym 15 minutes prior to the start of the game and stood near the baseline in front of the student section. This was an important place so that students and fans could see him in case an issue needed to be addressed during the game. The gym was over half full (more than thousand people in attendance) and most of the people in attendance were white.

As the game began, it was evident that the two best players on the floor were two Native American players, who were brothers, from Cityville North High School, the visiting team. They were quicker and more skilled than anyone else on the floor. As Cityville North High scored their first points of the game, a basket made by one of the two Native American brothers, the Cityville North High Student section, made up of 50–60 white students, cheered in unison, "Sa-vage Na-tion, clap, clap, clap clap clap" "Sa-vage Na-tion, clap, clap, clap clap clap" "Sa-vage Na-tion, clap, clap, clap clap clap."

To the researcher's astonishment, five white students in that section were wearing T-shirts reading Savage Nation. The researcher had not seen the T-shirts prior to the cheer and he took a second to take everything that was occurring. There he was, surrounded by over thousand people, primarily white, in the same gym hearing the same cheer.

He looked to see if anyone else felt a similar reaction to the cheer. Nobody that he could see felt offended, appalled, and embarrassed like he was and this created a dilemma for him. His conscience could not let the Native American community, especially students from both schools, be represented as a "Savage Nation."

Questions quickly rolled through his mind: Why was he the only one that felt this way? Why weren't there people waving for him to address the issue? Why was the administrator of the other school sitting there watching the game not addressing the issue? How will the students from the other team react when the opposing administrator says they need to stop the chant and change their shirts during one of the biggest games of the year?

The researcher chose to approach the Cityville North High administrator first and expressed to him that he did not feel that Savage Nation was an appropriate representation of the two student/athletes or the Native American population. He half-heartedly agreed. The researcher told him that he was going to let the students know they will have to change their shirt at halftime or they will have to leave. He said okay. The researcher was left to believe that the other administrator thought the enforcement might be appropriate, but not necessary.

The researcher approached the student section and identified what appeared to be a student leader in the group. During a time-out, he asked the student to come down and talk. He introduced himself as the principal of Cityville West and told him that at halftime that he and his friends needed to change the "Savage Nation" shirts. He asked why and the researcher told him that he did not think it was an appropriate shirt because of its meaning to Native American students. He said ok and went back to the student section. He talked to his friends in the student section and one of them signaled the researcher back to the student section. He said that he was not changing his shirt and it showed school pride for his friends who were Native American.

He said that if his friends did not have a problem with the shirt, then the researcher should not. He rationalized it by saying the researcher was just upset that his team was winning and the researcher's was losing. The researcher disagreed with him and told the student that if they wanted to stay after halftime he would have to change his shirt. He said "whatever" and returned back to the student section. As the second quarter progressed, the Savage Nation chants became more emotional and involved glances toward the researcher, almost out of spite. At halftime the students section left the gym and went into the commons and bathroom area. The researcher then spoke with the visiting administrator about the issue. He said that he had some problems with some of the students at past games and that he was not that surprised by their reactions.

At the beginning of the second half, only two of the original five students wearing Savage Nation T-shirts returned to the gym with a different shirt on. The other three students decided to leave. The Savage Nation chants dissipated as our team began to take over and eventually won the game (Davis, 2011). The racial advisor position in this group environment created some complexities not found in individual encounters.

First, there were two administrators who had positional power involved in this situation. Due to the location of the event, the researcher had more authority over the other administrator, but this created an odd dynamic. The researcher felt obligated to discuss this situation with the administrator prior to talking with the students. This may have created a barrier to addressing the issue if the other administrator would not have agreed with the decision to address his students.

The competitive game environment created a culture that allowed students to believe it was okay to refer to Native American student athletes as a "Savage Nation." The team was doing unusually well in the season and the star players were two Native American brothers. For a school administrator from the opposing team to address these issues with the students, the administrator would be positioned by the "Savage Nation" students as attempting to kill their school spirit as a way of gaining advantage in the game. It was also clear to the researcher that other adults in positions of authority at previous games throughout the year were aware of the situation and had not addressed it. This was not the first game of the year, it was about mid-season. The students had made T-shirts, which involve time to coordinate and cost to purchase. Their principal did not react to address the chants or shirts.

The other interesting dynamic is the public acceptance of the term "Savage" in reference to Native American basketball players. Prior to the researcher addressing the students, he did not have any person of the over thousand people in the gym that night talk to him about their opposition to the T-shirts or chants. The students were given a "pass" to use this degrading language due to the "support" they were giving their classmates. The public indifference to the terms "Savage Nation" at a competitive game in the presence of another administrator made the role of racial advisor complex in this situation.

The Savage Nation story is also a good example of the Critical White Studies tenet of Interest Convergence. Interest Convergence offers concessions for racial others that do not disrupt a normal way of life for white people. The white spectators accepted the success of the Native American student/athletes as part of their own identity. The student section or as in other instances a high school mascot allowed white students and adults to celebrate diversity by cheering for their team or their mascot. With the luxury of not being racial, white people do not see an issue using a derogatory racial name such as savages to describe their successful athletes.

The consequences for these actions are the perpetuation of negative stereotypes of a people who were stripped of their language and confined to reservations. Naming them as savages as recognition of the student-athletes success and hard work is inappropriate. The state of Midwest has addressed the negative stereotypes portrayed in high school mascots.

In 2009, Midwest Act 250 was passed "to allow a resident to object to the school district's use of a race-based name, nickname, logo or mascot by filing a complaint with the state superintendent. If discrimination is found, the school district will be ordered to terminate use of the name, nickname, logo or mascot within 12 months unless an extenuating circumstance exists" (http://dpi.wi.gov/pb/indianfn.html, retrieved on January 17, 2011).

This was the first law in the country to bar race-based mascots and team names in public schools. This story provides some evidence to the Critical White Studies tenet that whiteness is invisible for those in the dominant group. In a gym full of over thousand fans, mostly white, the sensitivity of race was absent. White spectators, not considering themselves as racial beings, led to a nonresponse. An entire group of people were being called savages and there was no response. Disguised as support, the references of savages to the athletes on the court and the Nation they represent became a socially acceptable reminder of their second-class citizenship, reinforcing long-held oppressive stereotypes.

As a white administrator during this game, the researcher felt like he was taking on a role of being the moral consciousness for a school community. In some ways, because he was new to the school community, he felt like he was able to move toward action easier. He didn't have a personal relationship with the people in the situation and his focus was on the racism that was occurring at the game. Since he did not have to make many administrative decisions about race at this school, it gave him some confidence to challenge the racism he observed.

The researcher also felt that the superintendent would approve of his actions because he had been in the district for four years prior to getting the principal position. In addition, he had done some work with racial issues as an associate principal at a previous school. His work on racial issues was seen as promising contributing to him successfully attaining a principal position. The researcher did not think his actions of addressing the crowd at the basketball game would put his job in jeopardy. In fact, the researcher felt obligated to address the racial issues because he believed this was one of the reasons why the superintendent put him in that position.

The researcher needed to work through his personal experiences of race that had developed a complex racial identity causing him to feel guilt and shame. These personal experiences caused him to react to the racism he was observing at the game. His racial journey began with his mother. She is a third-grade teacher in a small, primarily white Midwestern town. She raised four children to be respectful and compassionate, traits that one values. Her teaching style is similar to her mothering style, direct, soft-spoken, and doing the most she can to meet all students' needs. However, the researcher remembers his mother making comments about the inappropriateness of interracial dating. She would provide examples of some of her biracial students describing how confusing it is for these students.

Unfortunately, at the time, the researcher agreed with her and understood the racial code she was transcribing. As the researcher began to study Critical Race Theory and Racial Identity Development, he realized that one of the people he loved the most had created a racial lens that influenced the interactions he had with the students of color. It more so opened his eyes to how he was negatively serving nonwhite students. This realization created an unsettled "ambivalence" (Lensmire, 2010) in his understanding of self that needed to be resolved.

Thandeka (2013) describes the process of how white children develop a racial identity in relation to their own self-identity. She focuses on the damage that the white community does to its own children by creating experiences that force children to align with their race, even when they feel it is against their moral conscience.

These actions result in a compromised sense of self for white children, "I listened to several hundred Euro-Americans recount their early recollections of experiences that not only made them think of themselves as White but also taught them to act in ways that would keep them within this racial pale" (Thandeka, 2013, p. 10). Addressing the racist actions during the basketball game was a way to help move the researcher toward resolution with his compromised racial identity by creating a more racially conscious school environment. This was attractive and provided him with the courage to move toward addressing this situation.

As he reflects on this experience, he is concerned about being viewed as a white administrator savior who is willing to address racism as a moment of personal salvation without sustaining real progress in addressing racism in the school environment. He has searched for ways that school administrators, as racial advisors, interact with individual students and large groups to address racial oppression. In addition, he has pondered how to sustain racial dialogue that can generate more racially equitable school environments. One theory that comes to mind is Transformative Leadership as a foundation for school administrators to assist them in their role as a racial advisor.

Transformative Leadership theory can offer a basis for dialogue and action to generate hope toward an improved educational experience for all of our students. From a transformative leadership perspective, Shields (2010) explains:

> One must begin with critical reflection and analysis of social and cultural structures; move from critical understanding to enlightened understanding and action. Action will redress historical wrongs and help ensure that all members of the organization are provided with as level a playing field as possible—not only with respect to access but also with regard to academic, social, and civic outcomes. (p. 572)

This is different from more traditional transformational leadership theories that tend to focus on improving processes within the organization as a way to maximize success. Transformational leadership does not take into account our societal injustices, such as of racism. As students and staff walk through the doors of our schools, they are not washed of their social experiences. They bring these experiences to school, which needs to be taken into account in order to maximize learning. Everyone does not learn the same because we have different life experiences. Shields (2010) writes,

> The major divergence between transformational and transformative leadership is the former (transformational) focuses primarily on what happens within the organization whereas the latter (transformative) starts with a recognition of some material realities of the broader social and political sphere, recognizing that the inequities and struggles experienced in the wider society affect one's ability both to perform and to succeed with an organizational context. (p. 568)

Using transformative leadership theory requires a consciousness of the leader's role as a racial advisor, defining race in an organization as part of a larger societal issue that needs to be improved. This makes the role of racial advisor real and necessary to be a successful school administrator. This also embeds the role of racial advisor in leadership theory to provide strength in guidance as the role is developed and improved. To assist school administrators in developing and improving the role of racial advisor, the researcher offers two frameworks that have been developed to help define transformative leadership in a school setting.

Quantz, Rogers, and Dantley (1991) offered a framework of five "points" to organize dialogue for transformative leadership. These are (1) Schools are Arenas of Cultural Politics; (2) Organizations Must Be Based on Democratic Authority; (3) Transformative Leaders Should Come from All Levels of an Organization; (4) Transformative Leadership Requires a Language of Critique and Possibility; and (5) Leaders Do Not Gather Followers, but Help Promote Conditions and Discourse Which Cultivate More Leaders.

Shields (2010) identifies themes in her research that can provide guidance for exploration of transformative leadership within a school setting. These are (1) balancing critique and promise; (2) effecting deep and equitable change; (3) creating new knowledge and frameworks; (4) acknowledging power and privilege; (5) emphasizing both private and public good; (6) focusing on liberation, democracy, equity, and justice; and (7) demonstrating moral courage and activism (p. 573).

These frameworks for dialogue need to be studied and applied to real situations in administration preparation programs or professional development workshops for school administrators in order to be effective. Without a foundation for discussing race and racism administrators can be harmful despite having good intentions.

Using administrative stories like Meghan's individual racial advising or the Savage Nation case study allows current and future administrators with the opportunity to reflect on racism and multifaceted ways it can manifest in schools. The researcher recommends these points as a beginning point to explore transformative leadership theory as it relates to white high school administrators in their role as racial advisors.

CONCLUSION

Building on the foundation of Transformative Leadership, school administrators need to develop a network of support to be successful racial advisors. In this research, white administrators identified students, staff, and community members of color that they could have racial conversations with as a valuable resource to help discover themselves as racial beings. We call these people "racial allies." Each administrator in this study grew up in a primarily white community and learned their early racial lessons from white family and community members.

The initial interviews of this study showed this as a pattern in how white administrators make meaning of their whiteness. People of color (students, staff, or community members), serving as allies, to provide racial storytelling can help guide white administrators toward seeing themselves as racial beings and addressing issues of race in their schools (Davis, 2011).

Racial allies may also assist school administrators in resolving colorblindness by engaging them in storytelling of their racial experiences in order to make race a real concept that needs to be addressed.

Colorblindness was an acceptable perspective for some white administrators in this study. This position has the attractive appearance of keeping administrators neutral when working with students of color. However, the interviews also revealed the inevitable position school administrators are in as racial advisors. The racial advisor position forces racial dialogue that these administrators are not trained to lead. The conflict between a colorblind stance and a racial advisor position needs resolution.

The white administrators in this study pointed out that working with staff members of color allowed them to see a perspective of race that was not apparent without the staff member of color. The administrators felt that working with an ally of color provided validity in the eyes of parents and students of color while working through discipline issues at school. The allies of color can be important to provide perspective of a racial world as long as white school administrator's working with the allies of color use these experiences to inform their behavior.

The concern is the tendency for the white administrators to rely on these allies of color to address all of the racial issues that arise in the school. Unless the white administrators become aware of their racial influence and change their behaviors, the partnerships between white administrators and allies of color are insignificant (Davis, 2011).

With a theoretical foundation, Critical White Studies and Transformative Leadership, and a network of racial allies, school administrators need to establish a protocol when engaging a school community in racial dialogue. Glenn Singleton and Curtis Linton (2005) in *Courageous Conversations about Race* expressed the need for all members of the school community to be able to talk about race in a safe and honest way by designing *Courageous Conversations*. Singleton and Linton provide a way for educators to develop racial understanding, conduct interracial dialogue about race, and address racial issues in schools. The initial action for educators entering into Courageous Conversations is to commit to practicing Four Agreements:

1. Stay engaged
2. Speak your truth
3. Experience discomfort
4. Expect and accept nonclosure

To support the Four Agreements that define how we are to have conversation, the Six Conditions of Courageous Conversation guide participants through what they are supposed to talk about and what they need to be mindful of during the interracial dialogue. Consequently, the agreements define the process while the conditions outline the content and progression of Courageous Conversation. The Six Conditions are as follows:

1. Establish a racial context that is personal, local, and immediate.
2. Isolate race while acknowledging the broader scope of diversity and the variety of factors and conditions that contribute to a racialized problem.
3. Develop understanding of race as a social/political construction of knowledge and engage multiple racial perspectives to surface critical understanding.
4. Monitor the parameters of the conversation by being explicit and international about the number of participants, prompts for discussion and time allotted for listening, speaking, and reflecting.
5. Establish agreement around a contemporary working definition of race, one that is clearly differentiated from ethnicity and nationality.
6. Examine the presence and role of whiteness and its impact on the conversation and the problem being addressed.

These agreements and conditions are examples of racial discourse establishing an environment that allows white administrators to reflect and discuss the impact their race has on themselves and others. To prepare for the role of racial advisor, school administrators can use this protocol to work through a continual synthesis of racial storytelling, theory, and actions that will result in improved schools for all students.

This chapter detailed reflections and stories from practicing white high school administrators that illuminate their role of racial advisor and indicate a need for developing the use of theory and practice in our schools. The school administrator's role as racial advisors puts them in a dangerously powerful position to either sustain our historically racially unjust school institutions or move toward the hope of fulfilling our mission to serve all students. Through the use of Critical White Studies and Transformative Leadership theory applied to real-life examples with guidance from racial allies, school administrators can learn to be catalysts for change that will provide improved learning opportunities for all students.

REFERENCES

Allen, R. L. (1999, April). The hidden curriculum of Whiteness: White teachers, White territory, and White community. Report No. UD 033 097. Paper presented at the Annual Meeting of the American Educational Research Association. Montreal, Quebec, Canada. ERIC Document Reproduction Service No. ED 434 168.

Davis, B. (2011). *A case study of how white high school administrators make meaning of their whiteness.* Unpublished doctoral thesis. The University of Wisconsin-Milwaukee.

DeCuir, J. T., & Dixon, A. D. (2004, June–July). So when it comes out, they aren't that surprised that it is there. *Educational Researcher, 33*, 26–31.

Frankenberg, R. (1993). White women, race matters: The social construction of Whiteness. Minneapolis: University of Minnesota Press.

Grover, B. K. (1996). *Growing up White in America?* In R. Delgado & J. Stefancic (Eds.), *Critical White studies: Looking behind the mirror* (pp. 34–35). Philadelphia, PA: Temple University Press.

Lensmire, T. J. (2010). Ambivalent White racial identities: Fear and an elusive innocence. *Race, Ethnicity & Education, 13*(2), 159–172. doi:10.1080/13613321003751577

McIntyre, A. (1997). *Making meaning of Whiteness.* Albany: State University of New York Press.

Perry, P. (2001). White means never having to say you're ethnic: White youth and the construction of "cultureless" identities. *Journal of Contemporary Ethnography, 30*, 56–91.

Quantz, R. A., Rogers, J., & Dantley, M. (1991). Rethinking transformative leadership: Toward democratic reform of schools. *Journal of Education, 173*(3), 96–118.

Shields, C. M. (2010). Transformative leadership: Working for equity in diverse contexts. *Educational Administration Quarterly, 46*(4), 558–589. doi:10.1177/0013161X10375609

Singleton, G. E., & Linton, C. (2005). *Courageous conversations about race: Field guide for achieving equity in schools.* Thousand Oaks, CA: Corwin Press.

Thandeka. (2013). *Learning to be White: Money, race and God in America.* New York, NY: Bloomsbury Academic.

Chapter Five

Changing Staff Attitudes through Leadership Development and Equity Teams

Michelle Yvonne Szpara

INTRODUCTION

Changing the attitudes of faculty and staff toward minority groups in school is a key step toward eradicating racism and promoting equitable school environments. This corresponds directly with one of James Banks' multicultural benchmarks for school staff: "The staff attitudes and expectations toward diverse students are positive" (Banks, 2014, p. 128). Changing attitudes, including prejudices, assumptions, and expectations regarding minority groups, can be surprisingly difficult to achieve.

As first described by Allport (1954) in the *Intergroup Contact Hypothesis*, changing beliefs requires exposure to the "Other" as equals, such as in a service project for a third population, combining shared goals, cooperative effort, and institutional approval. Creating a schoolwide service project to meet these criteria can be an excellent, if impractical, means toward changing staff attitudes. Social psychology (Plous, 2003) provides other potential avenues for changing staff attitudes, utilizing exposure to accurate information about minority groups, combined with focused reflections on one's belief systems.

This chapter includes both current research references and hands-on activities for implementation in professional development programs for school staff. Each of the activities has been field-tested with in-service educators and other school staff. Given the sensitive nature of deep discussions around multicultural education, one suggests that educational leaders engage experienced staff development professionals to lead discussions, when possible.

While the focus of the chapter and the suggested activities center on promoting racial and ethnic diversity and creating equity in schooling around these themes, by necessity the chapter also includes examples of diversity beyond race and ethnicity. Diversity includes different religious and philosophical beliefs, such as atheism and humanism, diverse sexual orientations and gender expressions, differing language backgrounds, and more.

The overarching goals of this chapter are to (a) raise self-awareness among school staff of their own cultural understandings and misunderstandings and (b) to forge and strengthen connections among staff, to lay a foundation for long-term changes in curriculum, instruction, and assessment. Noel (2008) describes these goals as establishing a "community of practice." In establishing a community of practice for equity and social justice in the school, the following steps are suggested:

1. Beginning with self-assessment (for school leaders of all racial/ethnic backgrounds, and particularly those of White/European American backgrounds)
2. Identifying and developing leadership for equity teams
3. Assessing school climate
4. Selecting and implementing staff development activities
5. Continuing to develop change agents among staff

For the purposes of this chapter, school staffs are considered to include both teaching faculty, the myriad staff who support the school in various ways and administrators at all levels in the district.

CHANGING STAFF ATTITUDES: TRANSFORMATIVE SCHOOL LEADERS BEGIN WITH SELF-ASSESSMENT

When seeking to bring about a change in staff attitudes, specifically to identify and reduce prejudicial or biased attitudes among teachers and school staff, it is crucial to set an example through self-assessment. Whether school leaders define themselves as persons of color, individuals who are multiracial or multi-ethnic, or persons of White/European-American heritage, transformative school leaders need to assess their own racial identity development stage and their own mental list of potential biases. There are a number of ways to begin a self-assessment of racial identity understanding and implicit biases; the following are some possible suggestions:

• Complete three or more different self-assessments on prejudicial beliefs; collections of evidence-based assessments are available at websites such as these:
  – Implicit Association Test (IAT) collection, available for free from Harvard University (https://implicit.harvard.edu/implicit/education.html),

- Understanding Prejudice: Exercises and Demonstrations, available for free from the Social Psychology Network (http://www.understanding-prejudice.org/demos/; Plous, 2016).
• List your personal and professional biases, and formulate a plan to unlearn one of these biases.
• Analyze your racial experiences according to Racial Identity Development (RID) theories; determine your own stage of racial identity understanding.
• Seek a mentor from a different racial background than your own.

It may be tempting for efficient, multi-tasking school leaders to skip this first step, in order to begin the process of designing and implementing staff development activities for school climate change. However, engaging with this first step will maximize the outcomes that can be achieved in the school environment, by recognizing the growth process in the school's leadership first.

Self-Assessments of Unintended Prejudicial Beliefs

Utilizing several different self-assessments from Harvard University's Implicit Association Test (IAT) collection can provide thought-provoking results for personal reflection or discussion with a mentor. The IAT tests measure "attitudes and beliefs that people may be unwilling or unable to report" (Project Implicit, 2011, para. 2).

For example, is it possible that one might harbor unintended negative assumptions about a parent who comes to a meeting in hijab and politely refuses to shake the hands of the males in the room? Or one might be unaware of the depth of media-based imagery they hold in their subconscious regarding supposed connections between African American males and violence? The IAT tests were first launched in 1998, and a body of published research supports their use as a tool for understanding (Project Implicit, 2011). A similar, if less in-depth, tool can be found at *Understanding Prejudice: Exercises and Demonstrations*, available for free from the Social Psychology Network (2014).

Anti-Bias Work

Another, more challenging approach to examining biases involves making a list of your own conscious or subconscious biases. You can try making a list with sentence stems such as "Most (insert ethnic/racial group) are (insert adjective)" or "Many (insert ethnic/racial group) end up (insert outcome)" or "Many (insert ethnic/racial group) are good at (insert activity)." Again, while these beliefs may not dictate conscious, intentional actions, they may exist in your subconscious due to media, cultural, and familial influences. For individuals who are currently at an earlier stage of racial identity development, they may struggle with identifying biases or giving credit to the results of an assessment such as the Implicit Association Test.

It can be helpful in these situations to imagine personal involvement with individuals of diverse backgrounds. As an educational leader, you may consciously ascribe to an open school community that welcomes individuals of all faiths. On a personal level, however, you might struggle with the idea of a person of a different faith marrying into your own family, such as a person of Hindu faith marrying into a Roman Catholic family. Thinking of diversity in more personal terms can help to elucidate unconscious biases; these then become areas for future self-development.

Assessing Racial Identity Development Levels

For some individuals who have had limited experiences with racial diversity and discrimination, whether they are of minority-race or majority-race background, it can be helpful to examine their experiences in the light of psychological theories on RID. Janet Helms (1990, 1995) and Beverly Daniel Tatum (2003) provide detailed discussions of each stage of racial identity for individuals of African American and White/European American background. Racial identity involves how an individual perceives themselves as a raced being in the context of a racialized society. Racial identity development does not occur in a linear fashion; development occurs cyclically over the course of a person's lifetime, with a person moving forward or backward through the various stages.

Other researchers have developed related theories of racial identity development for Latino/a Americans and Asian Americans, as well as individuals of multi-racial and diverse ethnic backgrounds. Table 5.1 provides a brief summary of these models of racial identity, along with the source materials (in the Reference list). Additional identity development models have been postulated for individuals who are gay or lesbian, as well as heterosexual orientations (Cass, 1984; Wall, 1995); for brevity, these are not included in table 5.1. For individuals of foreign-born status in the United States, their experiences with culture shock (U.S. Department of State, n.d.) and cultural accommodation may be more relevant to their identity development than affiliation with particular native-born racial or ethnic groups in the United States.

It can be insightful to evaluate the relevant theories of racial identity to better understand your own interactions with individuals in a society that counts race as significant. Even if you personally do not identify your race or the race of others as salient, this may not be true for those you are interacting with on a daily basis. To analyze your racial identity level, refer to table 5.1 and identify one or more columns that you feel best represent you.

Table 5.1 Summary of Racial Identity Development Models

African American (Tatum, 2003)	Asian American (Kim, 1981, 2001)	Latino/Hispanic (Ruiz, 1990, adapted)	Biracial (Poston, 1990)	General Stages (Phinney, 1990; Phinney & Ong, 2007)	White/European American (Helms, 1990, 1995)
Pre-encounter	Positive ethnic awareness (family only)	Personal/family identity	Personal identity	Unexamined ethnic identity	No dissonance; racial identity is dominant representation in society
Encounter	White awareness/awakening to social and political consciousness	Cognitive dissonance and fragmentation	Choice of group categorization/feelings of guilt over choice	Ethnic identity search	Contact stage Disintegration OR reintegration Pseudo-independent stage
Development of positive racial identity	Development of positive racial identity	Development of positive racial identity	Development of positive racial identity	Development of positive racial identity	Development of positive racial identity
Immersion/emersion	Redirection to Asian American consciousness	Increased ethnic consciousness and reclaiming of identity	Appreciation	Deepening of ethnic identity	Immersion/emersion
Internalization	Incorporation	Successful resolution	Integration	Achieved ethnic identity	Autonomy
Internalization-commitment	Internalization-commitment	Internalization-commitment	Internalization-commitment	Internalization-commitment	Internalization-commitment

Within that column, choose one stage or two stages that you are transitioning between. Consider journaling about at least two different life experiences that support your choice. Analyze how your stage of identity development may work well or exacerbate conflict with someone who is at a different stage of development. This analysis can provide the basis for a fruitful discussion with a mentor.

Social Justice Mentors

Another means to self-assessment can occur in the form of seeking a social justice mentor. For the purposes of developing as a transformational leader for social justice, it may be most helpful to seek a mentor from an ethnic, racial, or cultural background different from your own.

This mentor should have extensive experience in social justice work, advocating for the needs and rights of minority groups, and have done substantive work on understanding their own (racial) identity development path. The mentor-mentee relationship should provide a mutually beneficial interaction, and both individuals involved should be equals in the professional setting. Above all else, the mentor should not be a subordinate to the educational leader in the workplace. Seeking a mentor in a demographically similar part of the country and connecting via Skype or other video chat venues may provide greater flexibility in identifying a suitable mentor.

Once a suitable mentor has been engaged, the conversations might begin using materials such as Tatum's (2003) "Discussion Guide" in *Why Are All the Black Kids Sitting Together in the Cafeteria? And Other Conversations about Race*, or the "Discussion Starters" in PBS's (2003) *Race—The Power of an Illusion: Discussion Guide* (Rogow et al., 2003).

Working with a social justice mentor involves the development and fostering of a challenging yet beneficial long-term relationship. Taking a few self-assessment tests online, such as the IAT, or making a list of subconscious biases and prejudices can be done in a single afternoon. However, the impact of these actions will be most powerful if they are combined with a plan for exploring and "unlearning" these subconscious biases. A transformative educational leader should develop a vision of lifelong learning with respect to understanding and working toward equity and social justice in schools.

As new biases are uncovered, a new plan can be devised to explore the bias and unlearn it. A caution that will be mentioned here as well as in the staff development discussion below is that subconscious/unintended biases can be as deeply entrenched as one's religious or philosophical beliefs. Research shows that implicit biases are malleable and open to change (Project Implicit, 2011); however, the process requires intentional exposure to accurate information about the group in question, combined with focused reflection on current beliefs and new information.

CHANGING STAFF ATTITUDES: TRANSFORMATIVE SCHOOL LEADERS BUILD EQUITY TEAMS

As demonstrated in the previous section on self-assessment for school leaders, the process of changing staff attitudes is lengthy and requires persistence. In order to bring about more pervasive change in the school system, it is helpful to explicitly engage a number of staff and teachers to serve as team leaders for long-term discussions and curriculum work groups. These "equity teams" can be built across professional lines, combining staff from the front offices and teachers from various grades and departments, or they can be silo-based, focusing on work groups with direct power to change policies for discipline or to change curriculum for specific subject areas.

It is helpful for the equity teams to include school and community members from diverse racial, ethnic, religious, language, and other backgrounds. This may not be possible, given the current make-up of a school and community. When explicit diversity is not possible for each equity team, school leaders should formally identify allies for each team, both as team leaders and as team members.

An ally in social justice work provides the "outsider" voice, to draw attention to and raise awareness about the concerns of a particular group (PFLAG National, 2012, para. 1). As described by *Straight for Equality*, a project of PFLAG (Parents, Families, and Friends of Lesbians and Gays, PFLAG.org), the voice of an ally carries power and credibility, and the presence of an identified ally can impart confidence to others on the team, to follow their lead and speak up for equity.

The first two tasks of the equity teams are to engage in the same process of self-assessment outlined for educational leaders above and to begin to assess school climate through a series of experiments, observations, and data analysis. Individual team members should be invited to choose a task for assessing their own stage of racial identity development and examining their own unintended biases. Insights can be shared in pairs first, followed by volunteer sharing in the whole group.

Team members should establish ground rules for safe discussions and should receive explicit reassurance from school leaders that their discussions within their equity teams will not be used for evaluative purposes (see P. Gorski's 2014 *Guide for Setting Ground Rules*, at edchange.org, as an example). Equity teams should be allotted time to meet throughout the school year, with appropriate management of their overall workload.

Changing staff attitudes to create more equitable schools requires the development of a core group of school members empowered by peer support and supported by school leaders to engage each other and the wider school community in difficult discussions of attitudes and beliefs about children from diverse groups.

School leaders should seek to develop peer leaders, among their faculty and staff, to empower both teachers and staff of color and to bring potential white allies out of the "closet" (Boutte & Jackson, 2013). By forging and strengthening connections among staff and faculty, transformative school leaders can lay a foundation for long-term changes in curriculum, instruction, and assessment. While the equity teams utilize their first several meetings for the work of self-assessment, they can also begin planning for the assessment of the school climate.

CHANGING STAFF ATTITUDES: EQUITY TEAMS ASSESS SCHOOL CLIMATE

In order to create more equitable and socially just schools, the attitudes of staff and teachers toward students of minority groups must be examined (Banks, 2014). Too often, students from minority groups are stereotyped as being less able and less likely to succeed academically, due to both overt stereotyping by media and cultural misinformation on the part of teachers and staff. When school curricula and standardized assessments do not reflect the lived experiences of students from minority backgrounds, they are less likely to forge positive connections between themselves and the school.

Transformative school leaders can engage the whole school in assessing where gaps exist between the institutional culture and the students' cultures. As described by Banks (2014), a basic first step involves assessing the cultural diversity of the staff, the students, and the community. Does the diversity of the school administration, teachers, and staff accurately reflect the diversity of the student body?

Consideration should be given to both obvious forms of diversity, such as race and ethnicity, and less obvious forms, such as religious background, sexual orientation, varying abilities/disabilities, and native speakers of languages other than English. When diversity is lacking, school leaders should acknowledge this in explicit terms and make plans to hire more diverse, qualified staff, as funding permits.

The next step in assessing school climate can involve looking for "-isms" in the school. Where does evidence exist for sexism, ageism, racism, linguicism, and so on? While individuals may commit racist or otherwise prejudicial acts against another person or group, it is equally important to examine evidence of systemic or structural discrimination in schools (Human Rights Commission, 2012).

Systemic discrimination can be difficult to identify in individual incidents and is more easily seen in collection of data over time. A school's equity teams might examine data for discipline records, looking for patterns in racial groups, types of infractions, and severity of punishments. Teams can also examine standardized test data, disaggregated by race, ethnicity, and other minority group identifiers. In both examples here, the goal would be to find little to no significant differences between the majority group and minority groups, whether in discipline processes or assessment results.

When systemic differences are observed, equity teams should engage the school community, and particularly those with direct influence, in discussing how to change the "systems" that led to this data. The systems are comprised of individuals who operate with relative autonomy but make decisions that affect the institution as a whole. This means that school security officers, teachers, students, and vice principals all need to be involved in discussing why male students of color, for example, might receive more in-school suspensions than would be expected according to the proportion of African American male students in the school.

The answer to such a question is rarely simple, and teams should plan to engage in in-depth examinations of factors both inside the school and in the community. Equity teams should work with teachers to examine their classroom practices, their assumptions about their students, and their skills in handling challenging classroom situations. All of these factors can affect the suspension rates of minority students.

In addition to analyzing school data for evidence of structural discrimination, equity teams should also interview or survey school populations for incidences of racial microaggressions (Sue et al., 2007). The concept of racial microaggressions has existed since 1970; it can be defined as subtle negative interactions toward individuals of minority backgrounds; the interactions can be verbal or nonverbal (Sue et al., 2007). Examples span a wide range of racial denigrations and can include ethnic or racial jokes or videos shared "for fun," comments about urban neighborhoods and their occupants, or overlooking the input of a staff member of a minority background.

The topic of racial microaggressions is rarely examined in depth, due to the difficulties inherent in its analyses. Transformative school leaders and equity teams can open the conversation on racial microaggressions to create a more open, empathetic, and inclusive school environment. An anonymous survey can be a fruitful way to begin collecting evidence of racial microaggressions, by asking members of minority groups in the school to describe instances where they have experienced negative interactions based on their minority group status.

All stakeholders should have the opportunity to participate in the assessment of school climate. If the overarching goal is to identify practices that negatively impact students and to create equitable school experiences for all students (Esmail, personal communication, email, 2014), then it is crucial to involve students, families, and community members in the process, as well as teachers, staff, and administrators. This can be done through anonymous comment boxes, a generic email address for input, open "town hall" style meetings, and other means.

CHANGING STAFF ATTITUDES: SELECTING AND IMPLEMENTING STAFF DEVELOPMENT ACTIVITIES

Once the foundation of self-assessment and climate analysis has been shaped by the school leader and the equity teams, the planning for staff professional development can begin. Basic questions to shape the planning of long-term activities for attitude change can begin with the following (add more questions based on individual school needs):

1. Does the diversity of the faculty, staff, and administration reflect the diversity of the students?
2. Does the school community include people from many different, diverse backgrounds—racial, ethnic, linguistic, religious, ability, sexual orientation and gender expressions, native-born and foreign-born, and other forms of diverse backgrounds?
3. Are there employees from minority backgrounds in positions of power?
4. Are there allies from majority groups in positions of power?
5. Do allies and employees of minority backgrounds regularly advocate for the needs of students?
6. Are advocacy suggestions heard, evaluated, and implemented where possible?
7. Based on the surveys of the school climate, are a majority of employees at higher stages of racial identity development?
8. Based on the surveys of the school climate, are a majority of employees able to understand their own unintended implicit biases?
9. Based on the surveys of the school climate, are a majority of employees able to operate in a conscious manner to overcome their biases?

The more "yes" answers that can be tallied in the list above, the more advanced the professional development activities can be, for moving staff forward in creating an equitable school environment. The more "no" answers that are tallied from the list above means that foundational work is needed to support staff in becoming aware of the structural systems of discrimination in which they unwittingly participate and benefit from and the roles they play as individuals in creating more socially just environments for all students.

As described at the beginning of the chapter, attitudes, expectations, and assumptions about cultural groups are extremely difficult to change, because they tend to be entrenched in our belief systems and remain unexamined. The positive news is that staff attitudes are malleable, with conscious effort and attention (Project Implicit, 2011).

Changing staff attitudes requires a long-term vision, with time for focused staff development, opportunities for personal and group reflection, and space for individuals at varying levels of racial identity development to make progress along their own paths to increased awareness. As discussed earlier, progressing through the stages of racial identity development does not occur in a solely linear fashion; the experiential and self-reflective work is cyclical and layered in its nature.

The following staff development activities are suggestions for planning monthly meetings over the course of at least a year to allow for sustained growth and ongoing discussions among school staff. Ideally, the transformative school leader should envision a three- to five-year plan for change, with staff development and engagement of the student body and the wider community at regular monthly meetings. Each meeting or staff development workshop should be 2–3 hours in length, at a minimum, to allow for substantive discussion, interaction, and reflection. Staff and student workshops should be led by trained diversity facilitators, in concert with the equity team leaders and identified allies.

If funds do not permit the hiring of trained diversity facilitators, the school leader can identify pairs of workshop facilitators from their own equity teams; the pairs should ideally be from varying diverse backgrounds. The workshop facilitators can review tips on setting safe spaces and handing difficult discussions from a resource such as Paul Gorski's *Guide for Setting Ground Rules* (2014). In either case, the school leader should allot planning time in advance of each workshop, with workloads adjusted accordingly.

Each of these suggested activities has been field-tested with in-service and preservice teachers from the PK–12 spectrum, as well as with college faculty. Suggestions for additional activities can be found online at http://www.tolerance.org/, www.edchange.org/multicultural/, and similar sites. The activities are listed in relative order of increasing "challenge." Activities should be selected to meet the needs of the staff at the levels identified by the survey of school climate and should progress over multiple meetings to higher levels of challenge and engagement with ideas of systemic change to increase equity for all.

EXPLORING OUR OWN MULTICULTURALISM

A good place to start understanding diversity and the "Other" is to begin by examining our own diversity. There are numerous variations on this type of activity; the main goals are to guide staff to list and share their own diverse cultural memberships. Cultural affiliations can include, but are not limited to, race, ethnicity, citizenship status, age, gender (not limited to just two genders), sexual orientation, languages, ability/disability, size, political or professional memberships, and hobbies and pastimes.

Staff should be invited to share their lists of cultural memberships within small groups and the whole group; sharing should not be required nor forced. An artistic variation on this activity involves asking school staff to use art supplies such as pipe cleaners or markers of different colors to create a representation of their multicultural selves. A challenge activity would be to first have staff share their creations; then ask each person to tear off or rip out a key part of their cultural identity, and throw it away. This can symbolize how some individuals experience the denial of key aspects of their identity, such as a gay teacher feeling that they must hide their identity from loved ones and peers, or an immigrant student feeling that they must hide their home culture and erase their home language, in order to be successful in school.

Workshop facilitators should remind participants of safe space guidelines and be prepared to facilitate discussions of the emotions that may arise. Questions for discussion might include the following: How does it feel to "rip out" a part of your identity? How does it affect your self-image and your sense of self-efficacy?

DEFINING AND APPLYING KEY TERMS

Once staff understand and accept the importance of validating cultural identities, both their own and their students' identities, then the group can progress to defining and applying key terms from the fields of multicultural and equity education. Small groups can take on the task of defining and applying key terms such as race, racism, institutional discrimination, prejudice, multicultural education, equity, and social justice.

Good resources for defining terms include chapter 1 of Tatum's (2003) *Why Are All the Black Kids Sitting Together in the Cafeteria*, free online resources such as Sonia Nieto's (2009) presentation on *Social Justice in Education*, and websites such as Teaching Tolerance (http://www.tolerance.org/) and EdChange (http://edchange.org/handouts.html), both of which offer free resources for both professional development and classroom activities.

Teachers and staff working in small groups can prepare formal definitions of key terms, as well as providing examples of these terms applied to their own school district. Creating a portable "word wall" of definitions on newsprint or an electronic composite of the groups' work can be useful for reference during later professional development meetings.

UNPACKING THE BACKPACK OF
UNEARNED PRIVILEGE

When staff have achieved a good grasp of key terminology in the fields of multicultural and equity-based education, it is useful to introduce and examine the notion of racial and cultural privilege. Workshop participants should read one or more resources on defining privilege (see "On Racism and White Privilege" on the *Teaching Tolerance* website or "Resources and Readings" on *The White Privilege Conference* website; the latter includes access to Peggy McIntosh's (1988) seminal article on "White Privilege: Unpacking the Invisible Knapsack").

Staff can then develop their own personal lists of ways that they experience unearned privilege on a daily basis. These lists can extend beyond racial privilege to social class or gender-based privilege to enrich and bring complexity to the discussion. A challenge-level activity can involve the school staff sharing their lists, and then "tallying" the relative number of privileges that different groups experience.

The workshop facilitators can engage the staff in examining how these unearned privileges provide different forms of social "leverage" or social obstacles to advancement and success. School staff can then apply their learning to questions of what privileges are available to certain groups of students and parents within their school district. An exciting and challenging way for schoolteachers and staff to explore notions of privilege further involves pairs of individuals from the school making visits to students' homes.

HOME VISITS

Home visits—conducted by teams of teachers and staff, arranged in advance with students' families—can provide deep insights into the lived experiences of the student body and can provide excellent background knowledge for creating culturally relevant pedagogies (see section below).

After school staff has examined notions of cultural privilege, as it applies to themselves and to others, the transformative school leader may choose to introduce the idea of making home visits. The overarching goal is simply to gain a better understanding of the myriad ways in which students and their families are culturally similar to the school's teachers and staff, as well as important ways in which they may be culturally different.

Visits can be as short as 20 minutes to introduce the school representatives to the family and to meet the family in their own home. The school may choose to use the opportunity to share information about in-school and after-school resources with families, or the visit can be purely focused on mutual introductions. Visitors may want to bring photos of key celebrations and traditions from their own background to share, and they can ask in return to hear about celebrations and traditions that are important to the student's family.

The school leader should not be surprised by teacher and staff backlash against the idea of home visits. Common complaints include the time investment and safety issues. Complaints and concerns can be used as a catalyst for deeper discussions about presumptions or assumptions being made about the students and their families and about the value of a home visit. The school leader can ask staff to brainstorm creative ways to bring the students and their families together as equals with the school staff.

Teachers or the school leader can invite the family to make a home video introducing themselves and their home, using a cell phone camera. This can be emailed to a central school email address or sent via a free service such as Google Drive (https://drive.google.com/) or Dropbox (https://www.dropbox.com/). School leaders and teachers should be sensitive that undocumented families may not feel safe participating in such an activity and alternate activities should be proposed.

For school staff who are willing to conduct even limited home visits (perhaps three family visits in one evening, once a month during the school year), the insights can be extremely valuable. Any information gleaned from family visits should always be shared only with internal school staff and always in a positive and respectful manner. Staff can be encouraged to hold one another accountable for presenting families in a positive light, with deep respect for diverse ways of raising children, creative ways of extending limited resources, and seeking a healthy balance across the multiple cultures of home and school.

UNLEARNING BIASES

Once school staff has been meeting for several months on the topics of diversity, social justice, and equity, workshop facilitators can introduce the activity of identifying and unlearning personal and professional biases. Readers can refer to the earlier section on self-assessment tools to help staff to identify unintended biases and to develop a plan to unlearn or reduce one specific bias at a time.

Biases do not need to be shared with anyone, but small groups should develop the means to hold one another accountable for antibias work. Resources and suggestions for antibias work in schools are available free online from *Teaching for Change* (http://www.teachingforchange.org/programs/anti-bias-education/articles) and the *Anti-Defamation League* (http://www.adl.org/education-outreach/curriculum-resources/c/creating-an-anti-bias-learning-environment.html).

It can be helpful for pairs of teachers and staff to share insights from their antibias work on a regular basis; the pairs should have no evaluative roles connected to their working partnership. The overarching goals of this activity involve the school staff working to actively reduce stereotyping, prejudice, and racism within themselves (Noel, 2008). It can be very helpful for workshop facilitators and school leaders to share insights from their own antibias work to set an example for others to follow.

LEARNING AND SHARING ABOUT DIVERSE CULTURAL GROUPS

In lieu of home visits, or as its own activity, the school's equity teams can engage staff in teaching and learning about diverse cultural groups, both those represented in the school district and those represented by the wider community (nationwide or worldwide). This multiday activity can raise self-awareness among school staff of their own cultural understandings and misunderstandings, and it brings the staff together to develop more nuanced understandings of the cultures of specific groups (Noel, 2008). Staff teams can choose or be assigned a specific cultural group; they are responsible for designing a user-friendly handout, brochure, video-log, or other presentation software to be shared with colleagues schoolwide.

The information in each group's presentation should include common stereotypes and accurate cultural information about their chosen cultural group; demographics and statistics on educational outcomes for the group; a brief history of the cultural group's experiences with education in America; and most importantly, culturally relevant strategies for helping students to maximize their learning. Many strategies that are defined as culturally relevant are also good teaching strategies for all students (Ladson-Billings, 2009). However, some strategies are uniquely appropriate for students from various cultural backgrounds. For example, students from some religious backgrounds may need accommodations in homework assignments for major religious holidays or may need supportive identification of certain food ingredients in the school cafeteria.

School staff can compile their presentations on selected cultural groups and add them to a printed or electronic database to be shared with new staff and updated on an annual basis. For school leaders seeking to share information across networks, an electronic database of culturally relevant teaching strategies, annotated with teachers' own notes from implementing different approaches, can offer an excellent resource.

TEACHING FOR CULTURAL RELEVANCE

A natural outgrowth of the staff's work on learning about the needs of diverse cultural groups can be translating this learning into lessons and unit plans based in the theory and practice of culturally relevant pedagogies (Ladson-Billings, 2009). The school leader can allocate time and space for teachers to work within and across subject areas and grade levels to analyze and rewrite curricula where necessary.

In the current era of prepackaged curricula, heavy emphasis on standardized assessments, and Common Core learning standards, teachers need dedicated time to examine and strengthen the connections between what is being taught and who their students are. The transformative school leader can provide regular co-planning time for teachers throughout the year to enact all or some of the following curricular adjustments:

- Designing and implementing culturally relevant pedagogies in both lessons and unit plans
- Rewriting specific lesson plans according to James Banks' (2012) Levels of Integration of Multicultural Content
- Examining how teachers' respective subject areas relate to current global issues (Noel, 2008)
- Developing subject-specific skills needed to take action on social problems (Noel, 2008)

The chapter on Equity Pedagogy in this handbook provides a more in-depth discussion of ways to strive for both fairness and inclusion in teaching for all students (see also OECD, 2008). As school staff continue to undertake the schoolwide charge of creating a more equitable, more socially just schooling experience for all, a natural outcome of this work includes determining which efforts are successful and which areas still need more work.

ANALYZING "BIG DATA"

The transformative school leader can initiate efforts among school staff to return to the original assessments of school climate (see earlier discussion in this chapter) to evaluate evidence for change. Equity teams can lead reviews of their original data, examining areas such as discipline referrals, attendance records, and standardized test data, each disaggregated by race, ethnicity, gender, socioeconomic status, and so on. Small gains might be seen on an individual student level, or the classroom level, when a teacher increases connections between the curriculum and the students or the teacher begins making home visits and contacting families on a monthly basis with positive student news.

These actions may translate into noticeable improvements in time on task, as well as reductions in discipline referrals. Teachers also need to continue the difficult work of analyzing their own unintended biases and assumptions about their students and invite peers to observe their teaching and provide feedback on raising expectations for students.

As school staff continue both individual and schoolwide efforts to support diversity, create equity, and teach for social justice, larger changes in student outcomes may be seen over multiple years. It is important to recognize that schools, while influential in students' lives, do not exist in a social vacuum. Transformative school leaders should also engage parents and community groups in meeting the needs of all students (see the chapter on Collaborating with Diverse Families in this handbook).

CONCLUSION

As school leaders and staff engage in concerted long-term efforts to create increased self-awareness and schoolwide change, advocacy and activism become part of the ongoing conversation within the school community. When staff repeatedly returns to work on unlearning biases, increasing empathy, identifying systemic practices that are discriminatory, gathering allies for change, identifying instances of microaggressions, and creating an environment of accountability, transformational change can occur.

As James Banks writes in Approaches to Multicultural Curriculum Reform (2012, p. 258), teachers are "an extremely important variable in the teaching of multicultural content." If teachers have the necessary knowledge, attitudes, and skills, they can become effective agents for change in improving schools and classrooms for all students. Because public schools in particular are subject to the control of many institutional forces outside of their own walls, school staff must also engage with the wider constituency of school-change allies across the nation and across the globe.

The skills of advocacy and activism (Wright Carroll, 2009) can be learned alongside efforts to increase culturally relevant teaching strategies and infuse multicultural themes into preexisting curricula. Taking steps toward advocacy and activism involves varying levels of risk, so it is crucial for the school leader to continue efforts to forge and strengthen connections among staff, students, families, and community members.

REFERENCES

Allport, G. W. (1954). *The nature of prejudice*. Reading, MA: Addison-Wesley.

Anti-Defamation League. (2014). *Creating an anti-bias learning environment*. Retrieved from http://www.adl.org/education-outreach/curriculum-resources/c/creating-an-anti-bias-learning-environment.html

Banks, J. A. (2012). Approaches to multicultural curriculum reform. In J. A. Banks & C.A. McGee Banks (Eds.), *Multicultural education: Issues and perspectives* (8th ed., pp. 242–263). New Jersey: Wiley. Retrieved from https://www.pcc.edu/resources/tlc/anderson-conference/documents/multicultural-banks.pdf

Banks, J. A. (2014). *An introduction to multicultural education* (5th ed.). Boston, MA: Allyn and Bacon.

Boutte, G. S., & Jackson, T. O. (2013). Advice to White allies: Insights from faculty of color. *Race, ethnicity, and education*. doi:10.1080/13613324.2012.759926

Cass, V. (1984). Homosexual identity formation: Testing a theoretical model. *Journal of Sex Research, 20*, 143–167.

EdChange. (n.d.). *Free handouts: Multicultural and social justice education*. Retrieved from http://edchange.org/handouts.html

Gorski, P. (2014). *Guide for setting ground rules*. Retrieved from http://www.edchange.org/multicultural/activities/groundrules.html

Helms, J. E. (Ed.). (1990). *Black and White racial identity: Theory, research and practice*. Westport, CT: Greenwood Press.

Helms, J. E. (1995). An update of Helms's White and people of color racial identity models. In J. G. Ponterotto, J. M. Casas, L. A. Suzuki, & C. M. Alexander (Eds.), *Handbook of multicultural counseling* (pp. 181–198). Thousand Oaks, CA: Sage.

Human Rights Commission. (2012). *A fair go for all? Rite tahi tātou katoa? Addressing structural discrimination in public services*. Retrieved from http://www.hrc.co.nz/race-relations/structural-discrimination-a-fair-go-for-all/

Kim, J. (1981). *Processes of Asian American identity development: A study of Japanese American women's perceptions of their struggle to achieve positive identities as Americans of Asian ancestry*. Unpublished doctoral dissertation, University of Massachusetts, Amherst.

Kim, J. (2001). Asian American identity development theory. In C. L. Wijeyesinghe & B. W. Jackson III (Eds.), *New perspectives on racial identity development: A theoretical and practically anthology* (pp. 67–90). New York: New York University Press.

Ladson-Billings, G. (2009). *The dreamkeepers: Successful teaching for African-American Students* (2nd ed.). San Francisco, CA: Wiley.

McIntosh, P. (1988). *White privilege and male privilege: A personal account of coming to see correspondences through work in women's studies*. Working Paper

189. Wellesley, MA: Wellesley Centers for Women. Retrieved from http://www. wcwonline.org/Active-Researchers/peggy-mcintosh-phd

Nieto, S. (2009, September). *Social justice in education: Preparing teachers for diversity* [PowerPoint slides]. Retrieved from http://www.sonianieto.com/ recent-talks-ppt/

Noel, J. (2008). *Developing multicultural educators* (2nd ed.). Long Grove, IL: Waveland Press.

OECD (Organisation for Economic Co-operation and Development). (2008). *Policy brief: Ten steps to equity in education*. Retrieved from http://www.oecd.org/education/school/39989494.pdf

PBS/California Newsreel. (2003). *Race—The power of an illusion*. Retrieved from http://www.pbs.org/race/000_General/000_00-Home.htm

PFLAG National. (2012). *Straight for equality FAQ*. Retrieved from http://www. straightforequality.org/FAQ

Plous, S. (2003). The psychology of prejudice, stereotyping, and discrimination: An overview. In S. Plous (Ed.), *Understanding prejudice and discrimination* (pp. 3–48). New York, NY: McGraw-Hill. Retrieved from http://www.understanding-prejudice.org/apa/english/

Plous, S. (2016). *Understanding prejudice: Exercises and demonstrations*. Social Psychology Network. Retrieved from http://www.understandingprejudice.org/demos/

Phinney, J. S. (1990). Ethnic identity in adolescents and adults: A review of research. *Psychological Bulletin, 108*, 499–514.

Phinney, J. S., & Ong, A. D. (2007). Conceptualization and measurement of ethnic identity: Current status and future directions. *Journal of Counseling Psychology, 54*, 271–281.

Poston, W. (1990). The biracial identity development model: a needed addition. *Journal of Counseling and Development, 69*, 152–155. Retrieved from http://www. ncbi.nlm.nih.gov/pmc/articles/PMC2695719/

Project Implicit. (2011). *Overview*. IAT Corp. Retrieved from https://implicit.harvard. edu/implicit/education.html

Rogow, F., Cheng, J., Adelman, L., Sommers, J., & Howard, T. (2003). *Race—The power of an illusion: What is this thing called race?* California Newsreel. Retrieved from http://www.pbs.org/race/000_About/002_04-discussion.htm

Ruiz, A. S. (1990). Ethnic identity: Crisis and resolution. *Journal of Multicultural Counseling & Development, 18*(1), 29–40. doi:10.1002/j.2161-1912.1990.tb00434.x

Sue, D. W., Capodilupo, C. M., Torino, G. C., Bucceri, J. M., Holder, A. M. B., Nadal, K. L., & Esquilin, M. (2007). Racial microaggressions in everyday life: Implications for clinical practice. *American Psychologist, 62*(4), 271–286. doi:10.1037/0003-066X.62.4.271

Tatum, B. D. (2003). *Why are all the Black kids sitting together in the cafeteria: And other conversations about race* (5th Anniv. Ed.). New York, NY: Basic Books.

Teaching for Change. (2014). *Anti-bias education articles*. Retrieved from http:// www.teachingforchange.org/programs/anti-bias-education/articles

Teaching Tolerance. (n.d.). *On racism and White privilege*. Retrieved from http:// www.tolerance.org/article/racism-and-white-privilege

U.S. Department of State. (n.d.). *Adjusting to a new culture: Culture shock.* Bureau of Educational and Cultural Affairs: Exchange Programs. Retrieved from http://exchanges.state.gov/non-us/adjusting-new-culture

Wall, V. (1995). *Beyond tolerance: Gays, lesbians and bisexuals on campus: A handbook of structured experiences and exercises for training and development.* Washington, DC: American College Personnel Association.

White Privilege Conference. (2014). *Resources & readings.* Retrieved from http://www.whiteprivilegeconference.com/resources.html

Wright Carroll, D. (2009). Toward multiculturalism competence: A practical model for implementation in the schools. In J. Jones (Ed.), *The psychology of multiculturalism in the schools: A primer for practice, training, and research* (pp. 1–15). Bethesda, MD: National Association of School Psychologists. Retrieved from http://www.nasponline.org/publications/booksproducts/multi_ch1_competence_final.pdf

Chapter Six

Building Bridges or Isolating Families

When School Policies Conflict with Cultural Beliefs, Values, and Ways of Knowing

María L. Gabriel

INTRODUCTION

This researcher has worked as a Latina educator for twenty years, and fifteen of those have been as an Equity and Diversity Specialist for public school districts in the Rocky Mountain region of the United States. She is also a mother of two culturally diverse daughters. Balancing the hats of equity educator and Latina mother of two daughters has given her many opportunities to analyze the ways schools engage with culturally and linguistically diverse (CLD) families related to school policies. As an equity educator and scholar, she has examined theories related to educational policies and research-based practical strategies for inclusive practice in schools.

She guides educational leaders in choosing, enacting, and maintaining equitable school learning environments as her professional career. Yet, as a mother of young children in the primary school system, she finds herself in a bind being on the other side of school policies that often are at conflict with her families' cultural beliefs, values, and ways of knowing.

As a Latina woman and mother, her cultural beliefs values, and ways of knowing are based in strong interpersonal relationships between stakeholders where diversity and the need for equity are acknowledged and supported. For example, she believes in building bridges to create strong communities between students, teachers, families, and school administrators for the success of each and every student. And, she knows that her ways of knowing are often misunderstood in the dominant mainstream cultural values of educational systems.

Because of her existence as a CLD individual, she knows what it is like to live on the margins, often as an outsider, to be excluded, and to have her voice silenced. Sadly, this has happened in school settings related to policy.

Having the background knowledge of educational policy and living on the margins has led her to sharing these experiences regarding inequities in school policies and the implications for cross-cultural communication that are created by the use of such policies. Writing from these unique perspectives models, the development and thought process of a critical multicultural educator and mother when confronted with school policies that often isolate CLD families.

EQUITY IN EDUCATION

Equity involves creating the real possibility for all students to experience high levels of success (Nieto & Bode, 2008). Educational equity is the responsibility of educators for supporting the high-level learning of all students, with thoughtful consideration and intentional increase to access and opportunity for students based on race, ethnicity, socioeconomic status, national origin, sexual orientation, age, religion, ability, and gender.

Achieving equity includes a variety of steps critical to dismantling the access and opportunities gaps, some of which include critically analyzing an educational system such as its policies, the inherent power in schools; recognizing that a cultural mismatch exists between most school leaders and their student and family population; and supporting increased access and opportunity to those who do not already have those advantages (Gabriel, Martinez, & Obiakor, in press; Klingner et al., 2005; Scheurich & Young, 1997; Viadero, 1996).

Through all of this crucial work, it is important to remember that relationships are key to building equity in schools (Cavanagh, 2009). Second, utilizing a critical lens to examine the inequities of school policies is the first step to moving toward equity for all students in schools (Gabriel, 2013; Gorski, 2013). Ladson-Billings and Tate (1995) offer an extension to critical multicultural education when they invite utilization of Critical Race Theory (CRT) as a tool to examine inequity in education. CRT has been described as a powerful and "hope-filled tool" to address the "achievement gap" that educational leaders are required to address in schools (Gabriel, 2013).

FAMILY ENGAGEMENT

Family engagement in most schools includes a traditional model of one-way communication that supports teachers in reporting information to parents at traditional parent-teacher conferences or school newsletter as the districts' key family engagement strategies. Often school principals will shift from sending hard copies of newsletters to families opting for an environmentally friendly online newsletter. Sadly, this eliminates a percentage of families from receiving the information due to lack of internet access or email know-how.

School personnel that have thought beyond this have worked with community partners to set up computer kiosks in community grocery stores and libraries or others that have offered computer classes to parents, so they can learn the database systems often held by schools where parents can access computerized information such as attendance, grades, and test scores. There are additional steps schools can take to provide inclusive family engagement.

Epstein, Coates, Salinas, Sanders, and Simon (1997) offer a model for increasing the effectiveness of family engagement by expanding that traditional model to include six levels of involvement beyond simply informing parents to decision-making and strong collaboration. When their model is addressed with a cultural lens, family engagement can be expanded to include the gifts of the cultures that culturally and linguistically diverse families bring to the school (González, Moll, & Amanti, 2005; Moll, 1992, 2010; Rothstein-Fisch & Trumbull, 2008) also known as "funds of knowledge," the resources students and their families have that often go unnoticed, unobserved, or untapped as ways of contributing to the academic learning process available to underserved students in public school settings.

The original pilot studies exploring the incorporation of the "funds of knowledge," funded by the W.K. Kellogg Foundation in 1990, included the assumption "that the educational process can be greatly enhanced when teachers learn about their students' everyday lives" (González et al., 2005, p. 6). González et al.'s work shares the opportunity for use and development of relationships between schools and families. "The guiding principle in our work is that the students' community represents a resource of enormous importance for educational change and improvement" (Moll, 1992, p. 21).

Nearly twenty years later, Moll (2010) reiterates, "For so-called minority children, especially in the contemporary social context, educational resources and opportunities must include integrating their language and cultural experiences into the social and intellectual fabric of schools, much as these have always been seamlessly integrated into the education of privileged White children" (p. 454). Studies have examined the use of funds of knowledge. For example, a study highlights fourteen Puerto Rican households with regard to funds of knowledge and finds the value of literacy in ways that have otherwise gone unnoticed (Mercado, 2005).

In another case study, it was revealed that twenty adults from the community participated in a funds of knowledge project contributing to the learning process of children. The funds of knowledge were incorporated into classroom instruction and were connected to homework, and both strategies increased literacy in English and Spanish (Moll, 1992). While not exhaustive, the included studies show how teachers and schools have incorporated assets, or gifts, of the CLD families into classroom practices, demonstrating how viewing, accessing, and honoring students' cultures as assets can bring positive educational outcomes and can impact the way we understand cultural beliefs, values, and ways of knowing in our communication of school policy as well.

SCHOOLS AND SCHOOL POLICY

Throughout the 1800s, and much of the 1900s, America's public schools were set up for reasons that included socializing immigrant populations (Moe & Chubb, 2009). Viadero (1996) speaking on the history of education writes that, "From at least the start of the twentieth century, one job of schools was to help assimilate the large numbers of immigrants flocking to the nation's shores" (p. 40). Teaching, curriculum, and instructional practice have continued to support the assimilationist perspective (Lindsey, Nuri Robins, & Terrell, 2009).

The trouble with an assimilationist perspective is that it insists on the exclusion and often degradation of diversity and minimizes or dismisses one's race, nationality, religion, sexual orientation, gender identity, gender expression, age, veteran status, family income, family structure, home language, and so on. The assimilationist perspective insists on a monoculture of Western beliefs, values, perceptions, and ways of knowing. Western academic institutions have accepted these assimilationist assumptions based in hegemony—those with power maintain ideas ingrained in the everyday thinking or common sensibilities of the masses and they evolve into perceptions that become natural and absolute (Gramsci, 1971). Over time, similar beliefs that have formed schools have also guided the creation of educational policies.

The federal No Child Left Behind (NCLB) legislation of 2001 was created to increase accountability while ensuring educational opportunities for all children (*Education Week*, 2004). Unfunded and widely unsupported, NCLB noted that, "Schools are accountable for overall student achievement and for the achievement of low-income students, students from each major racial and ethnic group, limited-English students, and students with disabilities" (Education Trust, 2004, p. 1). The legislation requires schools to disaggregate and report achievement data by the above-mentioned categories in K–12 grades. There has been varying responses to the reporting aspect of the legislation. Some believe that NCLB has actually left students behind as it has narrowed curriculum and has excluded those it most purports to support (Darling-Hammond, 2007; Gay, 2007; Hursh, 2007). An example includes,

> As evidence of its unintended consequences emerges, it seems increasingly clear that NCLB as currently implemented is more likely to harm most of the students who are the targets of its aspirations than to help them, and it is more likely to undermine—some would even say destroy—the nation's public education system than to improve it. These outcomes are likely because the under-funded Act layers onto the grossly unequal school system a set of unmeetable test score targets that disproportionately penalize schools serving the neediest students, while creating strong incentives for schools to keep out or push out those students who are low achieving in order to raise school average test scores. (Darling-Hammond, 2007, p. 246)

Others have welcomed the equity lens that had been much needed in educational reporting. McKenzie and Scheurich (2004) contend that, "Whatever the wide array of problems with the *No Child Left Behind Act*, it is, in part, a legislative response to the pervasive failure of schools and school districts to provide a high-quality education that ensures the success of all students" (p. 602).

Howard (2006) adds that when the data are disaggregated it forces us to look at who is being served at high levels in our schools and who is not. Achieving equity in educational outcomes through NCLB has become a hot topic that has affected educational systems at K–12 levels during the first decade of the twenty-first century. NCLB, previously known as the Elementary and Secondary Education Act (ESEA) of 1965, has encouraged a certain amount of accountability and stirred a general concern about how diverse students will attain the standards.

Yet without having a clear understanding of the role race, gender, national origin, sexual orientation, home language, and family income has in students' experiences in schools, the solutions will be one-sided—from a monocultural perspective. When the epistemological underpinnings of education are dominated by white perspective, it reinforces this monocultural perspective, because values, beliefs, and attitudes are tied to the thinking creating such policies and analysis thereof (Scheurich & Young, 1997). National policy is used as an example here to uncover the impacts of policy, and similar concerns exist in policies created by school boards and school administrators.

Over time, individual acts create or maintain systems of oppression and policies and support others in learning or unlearning the hegemony of school policies that exist. An individual can influence the structural and communication aspects of policy found in most preschool-twelfth grade (PK–12) school settings. Having practical strategies, tools, and time to reflect on the ways that school policy and the communication of such policies is cross-culturally effective or ineffective is a useful starting point for busy educational leaders.

To support this practical self-reflection, two types of policy will be addressed: *attendance* and *bullying prevention*. Both are related to behavior management and impact the success of students in schools. First, the context for each policy will be defined based on the school policy and communication of the policy that has taken place for our CLD family. Next, the implications related to the cross-cultural communication of each policy will be explored to further demonstrate the ways that a one size fits all policies and communication of policies has isolated a CLD family.

Questions and suggestions for school leaders to infuse a critical multicultural approach to improve the cross-cultural interactions with parents will be offered. As part of the discussion, a framework to review school policies will be offered for reflection and consideration by school leaders in the implementation, communication, or creation of school policy based on Banks' (1989, 2012) levels of multicultural curriculum integration.

Banks' (1989, 2012) model has been used to address multicultural infusion, and the author of this chapter has adapted this model as a means to consider being more multicultural and socially just in the creation, communication, and implementation of school policies to better support CLD families. The questions are designed to align with Banks' model (1989, 2012), so that educational leaders can see how policies impact their decisions in the context of social justice. The statements and questions in the table below allow for a reflective process to use in considering cross-cultural communication related to current policy implementation or can be used to reflect upon the level of inclusiveness of CLD students and families when creating policy.

The chapter concludes with final thoughts about the policy examples from a parent's equity hat and the opportunities for growth presented in the table from a professional's equity hat to support building bridges with CLD families in our schools.

POLICY #1

Attendance

Context. Zero tolerance, low tolerance, one size fits all, and punitive approaches to tardiness and absenteeism are policies and approaches found in many PK–12 schools across the nation. In the researcher's daughter's fourth-grade school year, she had not received communication about concerns related to behavior, academics, or attendance until the end of October. It was then that she received a mailed letter from her daughter's school addressed to "the parents of ... [her daughter]"; she opened it and found a computer-generated form letter regarding excessive school tardiness of which excerpts are included below.

Dear Parents/Guardians:

> It is imperative to student achievement that students are present for the entire day of instruction. Instructional time is a precious resource. Consequently, we view being tardy and leaving school early as a serious problem... . Being in school all day is important and demonstrates commitment to success... . Tardiness is defined as the appearance of student without proper excuse after the scheduled time that a class begins. Because of the disruptive nature of tardiness and the detrimental effect up on the rights of the non-tardy student to uninterrupted learning, penalties may be imposed for excessive tardiness.

To further build context for the way this policy impacted her family, she offered a deconstruction of the language found in the means of communication of the violation of school policy related to tardiness can support future culturally responsive educational leaders who hope, plan, and prepare to be more inclusive in the ways they enforce school policies with CLD families and to achieve equity.

"*... We view being tardy and leaving school early as a serious problem.*" Several years ago, a white female school principal told me that educational leaders need to hear from people of color. So much of their teaching and principal preparation comes from white middle-class females. It has resonated with the researcher and led to some of her best teaching. To learn that the school has a "serious problem" with one of her children via snail mail doesn't work for her. Culturally, she comes from a collectivist background where relationships are built on trust and time being in relationship (Trumbull, Rothstein-Fisch, Greenfield, & Quiroz, 2001).

"*Being in school all day is important and demonstrates commitment to success.*" Culturally, this language was perceived as an insult to the very being of the researcher. Success is measured in a cultural context. For example, while the dominant monocultural view in the letter demonstrates that success is time-based, the researcher measures success in caring for her children's needs. Without informing her of specifics, the researcher could only assume it had to do with the uneven number of tardiness between her two girls due to their orthodontist appointments. The researcher believes she is successful in taking care of her children.

"*Tardiness is defined as the appearance of student without proper excuse after the scheduled time that a class begins.*" We thought that a parent signature was a proper excuse, especially when we added in on the sign-in sheet that the "reason" is doctor, eye, dentist, or orthodontist appointment. When the researcher called the school to inquire about the logistics of the policy, she was told that a doctor's note was required to excuse tardiness. Culturally, it stings, as if it is a lack of trust, and one more hoop to jump through. I was also berated for not choosing appointment times that are not during the school day by a different school employee.

"Because of the disruptive nature of tardiness and the detrimental effect upon the rights of the non-tardy student to uninterrupted learning, penalties may be imposed for excessive tardiness." First, the language used in a form letter should be comprehensible and accessible to both parents and students. Second, the language feels threatening and isolates one by informing them of the gravity of the situation. Third, she was missing information. She would have liked to know the level of unexcused tardiness her daughter had received, what a proper excuse would entail, and what the possible penalties are.

Implications. The excerpts demonstrate deficit thinking; a trap that hinders achieving equity in schools in which the educational leaders point the proverbial finger at students and/or the families' internal deficiencies for educational failure (McKenzie & Scheurich, 2004; Valencia, 1997). A deficit perspective is described as one in which people are "defining students by their weaknesses rather than their strengths" (Gorski, 2008, p. 34) and becomes the way of understanding students.

Deficit theory has two strategies for reinforcing this worldview: (1) building on stereotypes and (2) overlooking systemic and perpetuated inequities (Gorski, 2008). Often these manifest as teachers' perceptions of inherent student deficits such as cultural inadequacies, lack of motivation, poor behavior, poverty, language, and families and communities (Diaz Soto, 2007; McKenzie & Scheurich, 2004).

> Often manifested in and within classroom interaction between teachers and students, these common assertions of deficits all lead to deficit thinking, blaming the victims for the shortcomings of the education system's failure to provide appropriate education for all students, particularly CLD students and low socioeconomic status, rather than considering such categories as assets or strengths. (Gabriel et al., 2016)

The deficit thinking illustrated in the letter further isolated the researcher as a CLD parent from her child's school, and the communication about the letter further removed her from a positive relationship with the school personnel.

Interaction. As discussed, the researcher was frustrated that this was the first time she was hearing of a concern in such a nonpersonal/formal way. The letter did not include any data, so she guessed that the reason why one child had received the letter and not the other was due to her orthodontist appointments—the only thing that differs in their attendance at school. When she called the principal, she stated that in her second year as principal, she had found that attendance was a significant concern for the school. She wanted to address it by sending out the computer-generated letters. The researcher suggested that she communicate in a more personal way if families reached the level of needing to receive a letter, but she said this would take too much time.

Questions to Consider. Considering goals of educational equity, inclusion, and acting as a critical multicultural educator, the researcher proposes some suggestions and questions to consider related to the policy and communication of the policy. First, it is unclear for parents what unexcused absences and unexcused tardiness is. Schools can support positive cross-cultural relationships by clarifying the systems in place in a variety of ways through paper copies in go home folders, email attachment, school website, and translations into multiple languages, or automated phone calls or texts.

What is the difference between an unexcused tardy and an excused tardy? How are they calculated? Do all teachers use the same systems? At what point is the computer-generated form letter initiated? Should data be included with the letter to detail the number of unexcused absences or tardiness? When should a personal phone call be used instead of a generic form letter? Should the message come from the classroom teacher or the school principal? Those are some basic questions to consider, but then it's critical to consider the unique differences in communicating policy with CLD families.

When a families' culture, including their academic background, experience with formal education settings, student and teacher relationship, and teacher and parent relationship are understood and listened to, new ways of interacting can and should be attended to. The current policy and computer-generated form sent to families such as this one uses a deficit theorizing model blaming the parent and threatening them and their children. It is written using terms and language that is highly formal and of a legal nature. It deters relationship-building and the creation of trust, which will likely not improve school tardiness or attendance, which was the goal. The intent of the letter did not match the impact of the letter.

POLICY #2

Bullying Prevention

Context. The researcher's children's school's discipline code includes the district policy related to bullying prevention and education and states,

> "Bullying is defined as the use of coercion to obtain control over another person or to be habitually cruel to another person." Bullying can occur through written, verbal, or electronically transmitted (cyberbullying) expression or by means of a physical act or gesture. Bullying is prohibited against any student for any reason. A student who engages in any act of bullying will be subject to appropriate disciplinary action including but not limited to suspension, expulsion, and/or referral to law enforcement authorities.

Another related district policy identifies the prevention plan including eight specific strategies, two of which are listed here:

1. To make reasonable efforts to change the behavior of students engaged in bullying behaviors
2. To foster a productive relationship with parents and community members in order to help maintain a bully-free environment

The researcher became closely aware of these policies due to her experience with the bullying of one of her children. A way that good intentions had negative impacts included the district's ongoing goal to find more eligible minority students in Gifted and Talented (GT) programs. In previous years it was determined that if the district cast a wider net the hope was that by testing all second-grade students using an identified assessment they would find students who were not otherwise identified.

The recruitment policy was implemented using a contributions approach, and thus the structure and context was unchanged but the existing net (assessment) was cast wider, not deeper. The impact was that by spring of second grade, students became grouped and then tracked. The identified leveled groups in literacy and math were static yet the students were not informed of the purpose, the meaning, the possible impacts, or the ways to continue to build community across this GT label. Immediately, in the researcher's daughter's group of four friends, they were divided down the middle. Two left the classroom for the pull-out GT services and the other two stayed in the classroom. Status was created and the friendships were determined based on the amount of time they had access to each other in the classroom.

In third grade, the conflict became a situation of bullying. There were small yet continual acts of exclusion and name-calling by the girl who did not want the researcher's daughter to cross the invisible friendship line drawn by the school systems' people and policy. Something that could have been avoided had school personnel considered culturally responsive strategies to address the classroom dynamics, including the culture of power (Delpit, 1988) and elevated status of students and certain parents, based on their GT identification.

The researcher went in to talk to the classroom teacher, met with the principal, offered resources, and specifically stated that the students needed ongoing opportunities to learn about each other to build strong relationships and caring for each other before they got older and found it harder to empathize with one another. In fact, the researcher offered resources such as restorative justice, which she knew were funded in the district. She couldn't get response or interest. In fact, the researcher was basically dismissed. The more she worked to advocate for her daughter the more she began to be left out of school volunteer opportunities.

Before fourth grade started, she contacted the principal and the classroom teacher to ask about their plans to address bullying between girls and alerted them to her concerns about the placement of girls in her daughter's classroom. She was fearful and went down the chain of command to solicit support. As the fourth-grade school year started, the same girl who had exhibited the bullying behavior began spreading rumors about her daughter. Then, she started excluding her in the classroom and on the playground.

The researcher's daughter told her about the experiences that often went under the classroom teachers' radar: rumor spreading, whispering, and "friend-stealing." She did not know how to communicate these issues to the classroom teacher, and felt betrayed when she sought out help from the school counselor and things did not get better. By the middle of fourth grade, she began to worry more and more about going to school, started talking about missing or skipping school, and stopped doing her homework. It was a difficult time for the family.

Questions to Consider. Considering goals of educational equity, inclusion, and acting as a critical multicultural educator, the researcher proposes some suggestions and considerations related to the policy and communication of the policy. First, it is unclear for parents and students what to do if they sense that bullying behavior is taking place in the school. Schools can support positive cross-cultural relationships by clarifying the systems in place.

What is the difference between conflict and bullying? What are the reporting processes and protocols? Are there a variety of ways to report bullying? What are "reasonable efforts" to change the bullying behavior? What do students and families do if they don't feel heard or responded to? Where do parents go if they feel that there is no productive relationship being fostered between themselves and school personnel? Has the bullying education included protected class status? Has the bullying prevention curriculum utilized an evidence-based approach? How have families been included in the messaging and the learning?

These are some beginning questions that school leaders can use to self-reflect on the accessibility of the policy. And, when educators are willing to add another level of being successful with CLD families when communicating, implementing, and possibly creating policy, they can be even more successful in building bridges than they were before.

The implications of mainstream policy and ineffective communication of such policy resulted in the isolation of a CLD family. The researcher's experiences become central here as she continually shifts between her professional and personal hats which she argues are founded and practiced on values and principles of equity, diversity, and inclusion. Advancing diversity, equity, and social justice are central to who she is and what and where she lives every day. She shares her experiences when facilitating trainings. As a CLD person and professional, she is always "on call" analyzing access and opportunity wherever she is.

These experiences she has shared to shed light on the need to be more culturally responsive and build one's equity literacy (Gorski, 2013) to have a more effective impact on engaging with families regarding school policy. The following table is an effort to support busy educators with an opportunity to reflect, respond, and affirm the diversity of CLD families in our schools when engaging with school policy implementation, communication, or creation.

Framework. This framework is provided to guide educational leaders to move up on the levels of multicultural benchmarks as adapted from Banks' model of the integration of multicultural curriculum (1989, 2012). While his original levels were created to support the infusion of multiculturalism into curriculum, the leveled approach offered in this framework can be used to guide educators in examining the state of and engagement of school policies. The questions are set in this table to demonstrate the ways that educational leaders can begin to consider their interaction with families in regard to a wide range of policies to plan inclusive affirming cross-cultural conversations about the expectations for behavior, attendance, academics, dress code, and other such topics that guide policies.

Utilizing this framework to analyze school policy with a leadership team will allow individuals to see what level they are at and where they would like to move toward. There are basic steps to consider being more intentional in reaching all families in a school through policy articulation. For example, a socially just educational leader will identify social problems and issues through the gathering of data and will reflect on that information to solve problems and resolve cross-cultural communication issues that arise that may negatively impact nonwhite students.

CONCLUSION

Rist (1974) spoke about the concern of public policy related to integration nearly forty years ago with important advice that we can learn from even today writing,

> Policy analysts will have to bring their background assumptions into the foreground where they can be examined and interpreted for what they hold as to the nature of white and non-white interaction, the rights of children, and, most basically, the nature of social justice. For in a society where opinions and power are grossly disparate, it is imperative the powerful and the powerless alike now the answer to the question, "Where do we stand?" (Rist, 1974, p. 63)

School leaders must garner the will to change school-based policy and practice so that policy does not serve as a barrier to educational attainment. Creating culturally responsive policy is a way to institutionalize the

Table 6.1 Critical Multicultural Approaches to Analyzing School Policies and the Communication of Policy

Name of Leveled Approach	Definition	Questions to Consider and Elements to Look For
Contributions Approach	Cultural components such as cultural heroes and holidays and discrete elements added to current policy and communication about policy, but the structure and context are unchanged.	Translation of policy into multiple languages has taken place. We highlight a cultural hero as part of our efforts.
Additive Approach	Content, concepts, and themes are chosen by mainstream stakeholders and are added to policy and communication about policy without changing the structure, purpose, or characteristics.	A focus group is held to ask individual CLD family members for their input and perspective. Their stories are not interconnected, fully described, clarified to the larger population, or impact the structure of policy.
Transformative Approach	Basic goals, structure, and nature of policy and the communication of policy is changed to enable multiple CLD perspectives to be understood and acted upon.	Culturally sensitive and intentional means of including diverse perspectives on school policies is invited and continually utilized.
Social Action Approach	Diverse perspectives are added and critical and reflective considerations are made to address inequities.	Engaging all stakeholders in thoughtful process and protocol related to policy is utilized. We ask ourselves, our staff, and families questions such as, "Are our CLD families part of our school family? Are our CLD students further isolated from educational access and opportunity with the current policy or communication of policy?"

Note: Adapted from Banks, J. (1989). *Banks' Four Levels of Integration of Multicultural Content.*

protection of marginalized groups. Culturally responsive policies would not allow biased harassment related to gender identity, race, ethnicity, and sexual orientation (Colorado Legacy Foundation, n.d.).

Studies have shown disparate discipline practices around the United States (Gregory, Skiba, & Noguera, 2010; U.S. Department of Justice & Civil Rights and U.S. Department of Education Office for Civil Rights, 2014). Policies will not be successful as a one size fits all approach as we consider the diversity of the students and the families we serve in today's schools. Good intentions can impact families in ways we didn't mean to when we choose large-scale interventions instead of more personalized approaches that take time and require that relationships be established and maintained.

Educational researchers have focused on four equity traps that have been found to limit equity in schools' policy, practice, and people to include "ways of thinking or assumptions that prevent educators from believing that their students of color can be successful learners" (McKenzie & Scheurich, 2004, pp. 601–602). The traps include the deficit view, racial erasure, employment, and avoidance of the gaze. Howard (2006) defines the deficit view and how it becomes an easy trap to fall into:

> From our assumption of rightness, we can easily conclude that our professional judgments are correct and that those who don't achieve, or don't perform in ways that are comfortable and familiar to us, are either not sufficiently intelligent or inadequately supported by their home environment. The deficiency, from this point of view, lies in the child or in the home, and not in the system of schooling or in the shortcomings of educators. (p. 119)

This quote reminds us to become more conscious of the ways we describe and respond to the diversity of responses from our CLD parents to our policies. As a professional equity educator, one has come to realize that the overarching message is that there is no "one size fits all" approach when implementing policy (and many other aspects of schooling). Varied approaches that take into account class, gender, race, ethnicity, sexual orientation (including gender identity and gender expression), age, and disability are necessary to ensure the advancement of diversity, equity, and social justice.

As an educator and parent, one has come to realize the importance of the application of culturally responsive practices that enforce the relationships built with families and students. Becoming critically conscious, eliminating our deficit thinking, and creating more inclusive learning environments can support our future actions in regard to many educational decisions such as, but not limited to, attendance, dress code, academics, behavior, and school bullying. Educational leaders are challenged to examine school policies such as those discussed, and their roles, practices, and consistencies in enacting them—hoping they will utilize these examples of interactions, the implications, and the suggestions to infuse a critical multicultural approach to improve potential interactions to further build bridges with all families.

REFERENCES

Banks, J. A. (1989). Approaches to multicultural curriculum reform. *Trotter Review*, *3*(3), Article 5. Retrieved from http://scholarworks.umb.edu/trotter_review/vol3/iss3/5/

Banks, J. A. (2012). Approaches to multicultural curriculum reform. In J. A. Banks & C. A. McGee Banks (Eds.), *Multicultural education: Issues and perspectives* (8th ed., pp. 242–263). Hoboken, NJ: Wiley. Retrieved from https://www.pcc.edu/resources/tlc/anderson-conference/documents/multicultural- banks.pdf

Cavanagh, T. (2009). Restorative practices in schools: Breaking the cycle of student involvement in child welfare and legal systems. *Protecting Children, 24*(4), 53–60.

Colorado Legacy Foundation. (n.d.). *Bullying prevention best-practices.* Retrieved from http://colegacy.org/resource/bullying-prevention-bestpractices/

Darling-Hammond, L. (2007). Race, inequality and educational accountability: The irony of "No Child Left Behind." *Race Ethnicity and Education, 10*(3), 245–260. doi:10.1080/13613320701503207

Delpit, L. D. (1988). The silenced dialogue: Power and pedagogy in educating other people's children. *Harvard Educational Review, 58*(3), 280–298.

Diaz Soto, L. (Ed.). (2007). *The Praeger handbook of Latino education in the U.S.: Vol. 1.* Westport, CT: Praeger.

Education Trust. (2004, Summer). *The ABCs of "AYP": Raising achievement for all students.* Washington, DC: Author. Retrieved from http://www.edtrust.org/sites/edtrust.org/files/publications/files/ABCAYP.PDF

Epstein, J. L., Coates, L., Salinas, K. C., Sanders, M. G., & Simon, B. S. (1997). *School, family, and community partnerships: Your handbook for action.* Thousand Oaks, CA: Corwin Press.

Gabriel, M. L. (2013). A practical and hope-filled tool to address the "achievement gap." In J. Brooks & N. Witherspoon-Arnold (Eds.), *Anti-racist school leadership: Toward equity in education for America's students* (pp. 93–111). Charlotte, NC: Information Age.

Gabriel, M. L., Martinez, J., & Obiakor, F. (2016). Dismantling deficit thinking through teacher preparation. In F. Obiakor, A. Rieger, & A. Rotatori (Eds.), *Critical issues in preparing effective early child special education teachers for the 21st century classroom: Interdisciplinary perspectives* (pp. 25–36). Charlotte, NC: Information Age Publishing.

González, N., Moll, L. C., & Amanti, C. (2005). Introduction: Theorizing practices. In N. González, L. C. Moll, & C. Amanti (Eds.), *Funds of knowledge: Theorizing practices in households, communities, and classrooms* (pp. 1–24). Mahwah, NJ: Lawrence Erlbaum.

Gorski, P. (2008). The myth of the "culture of poverty'. *Educational Leadership, 65*(7), 32–36.

Gorski, P. (2013). *Reaching and teaching students in poverty: Strategies for erasing the opportunity gap.* New York, NY: Teachers College Press.

Gramsci, A. (1971). *Selections from the Prison Books.* New York, NY: International.

Gregory, A., Skiba, R. J., & Noguera, P. A. (2010). The achievement gap and the discipline gap: Two sides of the same coin? *Educational Researcher, 39*(59), 59–68.

Howard, G. R. (2006). *We can't teach what we don't know: White teachers, multiracial schools* (2nd ed.). New York, NY: Teachers College Press, Columbia University.

Hursh, D. (2007). Exacerbating inequality: The failed promise of the No Child Left Behind Act. *Race Ethnicity and Education, 10*(3), 295–308. doi:10.1080/13613320701503264

Klingner, J. K., Artiles, A. J., Kozleski, E., Harry, B., Zion, S., Tate, W., ... Riley, D. (2005). Addressing the disproportionate representation of culturally and linguistically diverse students in special education through culturally responsive educational systems. *Education Policy Analysis Archives, 13*(38). Retrieved from http://epaa.asu.edu/ojs/article/view/143

Ladson-Billings, G., & Tate, W. F. (1995). Toward a critical race theory of education. *Teacher College Record, 97*(1), 47–68.

Lindsey, R., Nuri Robins, K., & Terrell, R. D. (2009). *Cultural proficiency: A manual for school Leaders* (3rd ed.). Thousand Oaks, CA: Corwin Press.

McKenzie, K. B., & Scheurich, J. J. (2004). Equity traps: A useful construct for preparing principals to lead schools that are successful with racially diverse students. *Educational Administration Quarterly, 40*(5), 601–631. doi:10.1177/0013161X04268839

Mercado, C. I. (2005). Seeing what's there: Language and literacy funds of knowledge in New York Puerto Rican homes. In A. C. Zentella (Ed.), *Building on strength: Language and literacy in Latino families and communities* (pp. 134–147). New York, NY: Teachers College Press.

Moe, T. M., & Chubb, J. E. (2009). *Liberating learning: Technology, politics, and the future of American education.* San Francisco, CA: Jossey-Bass.

Moll, L. C. (1992). Bilingual classroom studies and community analysis: Some recent trends. *Educational Researcher, 21*(2), 20–24.

Moll, L. C. (2010). Mobilizing culture, language, and educational practices. *Educational Researcher, 39*(6), 451–460. doi:10.3102/0013189X10380654

Nieto, S., & Bode, P. (2008). *Affirming diversity: The sociopolitical context of multicultural education* (5th ed.). San Francisco, CA: Pearson Education.

Rist, R. C. (1974). Race, policy and schooling. *Society, 12*(1), 59–63.

Rothstein-Fisch, C., & Trumbull, E. (2008). *Managing diverse classrooms: How to build on students' cultural strengths.* Alexandria, VA: Association for Supervision and Curriculum Development.

Scheurich, J. J., & Young, M. D. (1997, May). Coloring epistemologies: Are our research epistemologies racially biased? *Educational Researcher, 26*(4), 4–16.

Trumbull, E., Rothstein-Fisch, C., Greenfield, P. M., & Quiroz, B. (2001). *Bridging cultures between home and school: A guide for teachers with a special focus on immigrant Latino families.* Mahwah, NJ: Lawrence Erlbaum.

U.S. Department of Justice & Civil Rights. (2014, January 8). *On the nondiscriminatory administration of school discipline.* Retrieved from http://www2.ed.gov/about/offices/list/ocr/letters/colleague-201401-title-vi.html

Valencia, R. R. (Ed.). (1997). *The evolution of deficit thinking: Educational thought and practice.* Washington, DC: Falmer Press.

Viadero, D. (1996, April 10). Culture clash. *Education Week, 15*(29), 39–42.

Chapter Seven

Principals, School Climate, and Social Justice

How State Compliance with National Initiatives May Not Be Enough

Susan L. Dodd

INTRODUCTION

In an age where there is more support than ever from state and federal governments for improving school climate there is also more accountability for school administrators in ensuring that the attitudes of school staff are conducive to teaching and learning (Thapa, Cohen, Higgins-D'Alessandro, & Guffy, 2012). In this chapter, we discuss compliance issues in the state of New York to generalize how these initiatives may not go far enough in promoting social justice. New York State follows national initiatives for defining school climate as, "the quality and character of school life" (NYSED, 2013; Piscatelli & Lee, 2011).

In New York, as in many other states, schools must demonstrate how the issues of school climate and student well-being are addressed through codes of conduct and schoolwide initiatives, such as character education programs and Positive Behavioral Interventions and Supports (PBIS, 2014). However, there are no state requirements for evaluating the effectiveness of these school climate strategies. Furthermore, despite research on the importance of emotional connectedness within schools, as will be outlined below, school climate is often assessed in terms of observable behaviors, such as the number of discipline referrals.

This chapter will address one recent reform, the Dignity for All Students Act (also referred to as the Dignity Act or DASA), which aims to eradicate behaviors of social injustice, but does not require schools to evaluate the attitudes leading to those behaviors. After a brief overview of the literature on first- and second-order change, the Dignity Act will be positioned as a first-order change, as it does not require an examination of underlying ideologies that may implicitly support acts of discrimination.

The first part of this chapter highlights the concept of connectedness as it relates to school climate. This is followed by a brief review of national initiatives and state mandates for school climate that many school administrators are now working under. The remainder of this chapter will focus on the need for administrator preparation programs to explicitly train future principals on how to implement and assess school climate programs that foster connectedness for all students. In response to the lack of research regarding models of principal preparation in this domain, this chapter concludes with specific examples of strategies and training activities to help foster educator awareness on topics such as personal bias and cultural sensitivity.

SCHOOL CLIMATE AND CONNECTEDNESS

Significant research studies have found that a positive school climate is often associated with factors such as higher teacher satisfaction, higher academic achievement, lower dropout rates, and fewer discipline referrals (Blum, 2005; Thapa et al., 2012). As part of a school climate that is welcoming of all student backgrounds, there is a strong positive correlation between academic success and having interpersonal connections between students and school staff (Blum, 2005; Cohen, McCabe, Michelli, & Pickeral, 2009; Faster & Lopez, 2013; Thapa et al., 2012). These connections, such as the amount of care and support students perceive to have from their teachers, impact the level of engagement that students display in their classroom efforts (Blum, 2005; Osher, Spier, Kendziora, & Cai, 2009). Learning is grounded in the ways students of various cultural backgrounds learn to speak and interact with each other.

Despite an abundance of evidence linking a positive school climate to improved outcomes on various levels, there is a disconnection in the actual implementation of comprehensive reform (Borman, Hewes, Overman, & Brown, 2003; Cohen et al., 2009; Haynes, Emmons, & Woodruff, 1998).

NATIONAL SCHOOL CLIMATE REFORM

Although the topic of school climate has been under review for over a century (National School Climate Council, 2007), it is only in recent years that specific guidelines have been established to directly address the need for a purposeful and cohesive atmosphere of respect and collaboration. It can easily be assumed that one reason for the heightened attention to creating positive school climates is in reaction to the widespread media attention on instances of bullying and violence within schools. However, the question of what constitutes a "positive" school climate becomes muddled because, just as there is no universally agreed upon definition for bullying, the term school climate has also yet to be operationalized (Cohen et al., 2009).

When adding in the component of social justice to school climate, the definition becomes even more nebulous because individual interpretations of this term also vary widely. In one study where school administrators were asked to share their perspectives on the meaning of social justice, the responses were wide ranging and divided (Jenlink & Jenlink, 2012). The authors of this study concluded that part of the reason why responses ranged from very general and vague notions of "fairness" to more complex notions of systematic inequality is due to the fact that perspectives of social justice are not often openly discussed among administrators or within schools (Jenlink & Jenlink, 2012).

This lack of discourse and implicit acceptance of any prevailing inequities hinder the opportunities for self-reflection and careful analysis of institutional inequities. Although most administrators are in support of creating a positive school climate, many are left searching for guidelines in how this is to be accomplished (Cohen, 2014). When a term such as school climate is open for interpretation, it is more likely that the school's atmosphere, policies, and cohesiveness will reflect the norms and values of the dominant culture rather than serve the needs of all stakeholders.

The lack of a universal definition is also troublesome now that many administrators are being asked to provide evidence of school climate reforms within their districts, a change resulting from an increase in the amount of attention paid by state and federal agencies to the need for a positive school climate. A scan of state policies throughout the nation in 2007 revealed that most state and district-level policies made no mention of any research-based guidelines to improve school climate (National School Climate Council, 2007). Since that time, many states, such as New York, have updated their policies to include quantitative measures of behavior.

THE DIGNITY FOR ALL STUDENTS ACT

The New York State Education Department has recently passed the Dignity for All Students Act, which provides that students must be able to attend school in an environment that is free of harassment from school staff and other students. The protected areas include perceived race, color, weight, national origin, ethnic group, religion, religious practice, disability, sexual orientation, gender (including gender identity), or sex. These are also the most common targets for both bullying and cyberbullying (NSCC, 2007), with homophobic-based behaviors being especially problematic in terms of bullying and harassment (Birkett, Espelage, & Koenig, 2009). As part of the mandatory compliance with this act, administrators must ensure that their schools have a plan for a positive school climate that promotes the safety and well-being of the students (NYSED, 2013). However, there are no requirements that the plan be evaluated for effectiveness, nor to fundamentally change the attitudes leading to aggressive actions.

As with many other school reform mandates, a new program is implemented with the intention of creating change, yet the new policies are merely assimilated into an existing structure of norms, values, and beliefs that do not undergo any significant evaluation or change. Hesbol (2013) delineates the concepts of first- and second-order change, as they relate to school reform and building inclusive communities. In a first-order change, policies are enacted with no examination of institutional practices that silently promote one form of being over another, whereas a second-order change requires a major systems appraisal, where policies and norms are evaluated and restructured to fit the needs of all constituents (Hesbol, 2013).

Given that the Dignity Act does not create a need for disruption of the overall structure of schools, nor do the new guidelines for rewriting Codes of Conduct compel administrators to examine their own worldviews, this mandate is reflective of a first-order change. Without a major shift in the structures that allow racism and bias to continue, the focus will remain on rules for desired behaviors, rather than questioning the belief structures that lead to acts of discrimination.

After its first year of inception, the Dignity Act was amended with a requirement for all preservice educators to attend a six-hour workshop that includes information on topics such as understanding diversity and personal bias and developing sensitivity to the experiences of specific student populations. Other aspects of the training outline the impact of school climate on student achievement and behavior and the power of language and its role in prevention and intervention.

For many administrators, this may be the only time in their careers when issues of "diversity" are directly discussed. While it may be a step in the right direction, this workshop does not allow enough time for participants to self-examine their long-held beliefs, nor does the workshop provide adequate training on how to reform the existing culture of a school. However, the guidelines for DASA trainings focus on the development of interpersonal empathy as a way for educators to connect with all students and gain an understanding of the obstacles that many students face. The most logical place to begin thinking about and discussing issues of social justice and how they come into play within a school setting is in teacher and administrator preparation programs, with mandates to involve current educators in additional hours of continuing education.

ADMINISTRATOR PREPARATION PROGRAMS

It has been said, "We can't teach what we don't know" (Howard, 1999). The same can be said for administrators who are trying to demonstrate an understanding of concepts that they've never deeply considered. Because administrators are so pivotal in setting the tone for expectations and attitudes within the school, and because student success and teacher satisfaction are so closely connected to school climate, it is essential that administrators are well prepared to lead a school staff by example and by modeling behaviors that are democratic and respectful.

However, as with every other person in the building and community, principals hold a lifetime of values, ideas, and perspectives that have been shaped by existence in a society where inequalities are often not discussed openly, especially in a public school forum. From a social reconstructivist perspective, it is argued that every element of education exists within a cultural context that informs the practices of the people within (Agosto, Dias, Kaiza, McHatton, & Elam, 2013). Contextualizing schools within this ecological framework, where the inherent beliefs, attitudes, and expectations for behavioral norms are deeply embedded within the fabric of the system, it is necessary that principals are provided with an opportunity to recognize that their positions as leaders are culturally informed.

Preparation for this element of school leadership should be purposeful and handled with the same regard as are others aspects of school administration, with all aspects of schooling and education considered within the praxis of social justice issues. Many people from the dominant white and middle-class culture, as are most administrators, have reached young adulthood without ever questioning the racial and classist biases entrenching most aspects of American society (King, 1991). Professors of Educational Leadership need to assist future school administrators in increasing their self-awareness of how their race, gender, class, ability, religion, and sexual orientation all influence who they are as leaders, as well as recognizing their power and responsibility to notice and to challenge inequities within their schools.

This educational process is both practical and philosophical in nature, and it may be an aspect of leadership that many current and future educators have never deeply considered. Unfortunately, administrator preparation programs across the nation are inconsistent in their approach to discussing issues of school climate and social justice and have remained static despite the increased state and national attention given to social justice reformation

(Agosto et al., 2013; Byrne-Jiménez & Orr, 2013; Hesbol, 2013; Reis & Smith, 2013).

It is a complex task for school administrators to not only understand their own belief structures but also assess their school community within the contexts of time, location, history, and culture. It is therefore imperative that administrators are not only trained in effective multicultural pedagogy but also able to convey these expectations to teachers in measurable terms. Ideally, this would happen in a way that does not merely include individual teaching strategies, but would change schoolwide attitudes and policies that may be interfering with teaching and learning.

School data can be used as a springboard for discussions on issues of educational equity and practices and beliefs that should be scrutinized for areas of injustice (Hesbol, 2013). Administrators should be prepared for the intricate and often thorny terrain of school leadership, particularly when it comes to challenging practices that have long been in place. It is imperative that administrators understand that there are institutional structures in place that benefit some students and not others and that the school staff has an obligation to restructure these areas of inequity.

Students experience the elements of power and privilege embedded within school practices and other environments on a daily basis. Extending beyond the mandates to eliminate name-calling and other forms of harassment, administrators need to consider and critique the wider aspects of schooling and the impact this has on both students and teachers. Preservice educators can begin to practice a stance of critical inquiry in regard to school-based policies that might not favor all students.

Ideally, this learning could take place in collaboration with practicing administrators who are willing to spend time partnering with administrator preparation programs. Even a decade prior to DASA, it was noted that administrators do not create a school's atmosphere in a vacuum, partnerships are necessary for the improvement climate, and this type of collaboration can benefit everyone involved (Herrity & Glassman, 2010).

IMPLEMENTING A POSITIVE SCHOOL CLIMATE

New York State schools now must provide evidence of a research-based school climate initiative, such as PBIS. Here again, the language and concepts get confusing. PBIS can be used as an effective tool within a greater arena of school climate reform. However, in and of itself, PBIS is a behavioristic approach that relies on extrinsic motivators and rewards for positive behavior, rather than instilling a more complex understanding of systematic inequalities (Cohen, 2014).

Focusing on a purely behavioral approach minimizes the likelihood that students will develop an inherent respect for others, in favor of following rules for good behavior and potential reward. The mandate for the DASA compliance and the accompanying updates for student handbooks specify clearly delineated guidelines for unacceptable behavior, and there is evidence that a climate reform such as PBIS can help reduce discipline referrals, but the program is touted as "effective discipline for student success" (PBIS, 2014). Students and educators can easily be trained to follow these rules, but this is a very individualized approach to social justice and it does not require anyone to question elements of inequality within the school beyond behavioral interactions.

Where in this system of discipline are the conversations around equity, systematic racism, and other forms of bias that hinder success and well-being? These prescriptions for behavior then become just another set of rules and management that is cut off from a more holistic understanding of the underlying forces of inequity (Mullen, 2011). Are schools on the one hand promoting a desire for good behavior in the form of respecting others but, on the other hand, employing policies and practices that are inequitable?

Despite the fact that student harassment in any of the protected areas is not tolerated, in what ways are white, middle class, hetero, Christian, and athletic norms/values promoted? So much about a school's climate can be felt when walking into the building, and administrators have complete control over setting this tone. Whose pictures are hanging in the hallway? What artifacts are presented in display cases throughout the school? Are all types of students represented in these very visual statements of who adds value to the school environment?

These are the deeper questions that a program such as PBIS might not address. Again, to go beyond the basic requirement of implementing a "positive school climate" to be in compliance with DASA regulations, building leaders can work toward effective change by addressing the attitudes and not just the actions of the school staff. The remaining question is how can principals who have limited or no specific training in the area of cultural competence pass these values to others?

New York's DASA training is a good first step, but even there lie vast differences in how the trainings are conducted. DASA workshop conductors are given a very open-ended curriculum to cover the topic of "Understanding diversity, personal bias & developing sensitivity to the experiences of specific student populations" (NYSED, 2013). A targeted training for all preservice educators alleviates some of the burden from administrators who must take it upon themselves to act as change-agents within their schools. However, this type of training is state-specific, and there are many states that do not require such training for certification. Likewise, despite a plethora of research-based

tools for measuring school climate, most states don't require any such measurement and remain open-ended in their definitions of this concept (Safe
Supportive Learning, 2014).

MEASURING SCHOOL CLIMATE

In an effort to make concepts measurable, it is easy to become over-reliant
on simple sources of data collection, such as discipline referrals. However,
to truly measure the attitudes and perceptions of teachers, students, and other
stakeholders, it is necessary to have a more comprehensive evaluation system in place. Despite an existence of valuable tools that have already been
assessed for measuring these elements as a part of school climate reform, most
states do not require any such evaluation (Safe Supportive Learning, 2014).

In fact, in the aforementioned policy scan (Piscatelli & Lee, 2011), it was
determined that most states held very ill-defined concepts of school climate
and used terms that are open for interpretation and not easily measured.
Logically, if an instrument used to measure aspects of school climate is constructed in a way that could be understood differently by the survey respond-
ents, the form of assessment is a great waste of time and energy. Although
many states now require schools to adopt a school climate initiative, however
defined, only Rhode Island requires states to measure school climate using a
tool that has been formally verified as valid and reliable (Cohen, 2014).

Instrument validity is crucial for administrators to get a real measure for
whether their perceptions are matched by other stakeholders and if there is a
shared understanding of and an agreement on the needs of the school. From
there, this data can be a guiding point for setting goals and establishing priorities within the school or district (Safe Supportive Learning, 2014).

The context of the assessments used can also help frame approaches to
ensuring issues of equity and social justice within the overall climate of the
school. Gaining essential feedback on relevant issues from all stakeholders
ensures that all voices have a chance to be heard and it provides the school
leader with an opportunity to ensure teachers and other members of the
school community that their perspectives are valued in a tangible way (Faster
& Lopez, 2013).

CONCLUSION

The strategies and suggestions here are double-sided; any recommendations
for changes in behavior should be concurrent with a greater sense of awareness and an action-oriented approach toward equity. School leaders will
need to deeply consider their own perspectives before attempting to alter the

attitudes of staff or anyone else. It is important for school leaders to openly contextualize what it means to be in a position of privilege and understand the impact that their worldview has on the school community. An ideal place to start is to formally assess the school climate and at least operationalize the terms and concepts the school community would like to measure. A school climate committee composed of diverse stakeholders could seek out a scientifically sound assessment tool that would work well for their specific population.

As previously mentioned, empathy training can be a valuable component in extending beyond a behavioral approach to social justice. When a school leader takes time at staff meetings to talk about school climate, faculty and staff will understand that this is valued. Group activities such as "Inclusion/ Exclusion" (EdChange, 2014) can help faculty recall their own days of schooling and remember what felt good for them, what didn't, and why. With an abundance of evidence that a sense of connectedness at school is beneficial in so many ways, it is necessary to take time out and reflect on whether or not these connections are being made with all students and staff on a regular basis.

Part of this transformation might be to encourage meaningful connections between staff and students, such as a check-in program where each staff member is responsible for touching base with a given number of students outside of the classroom. School staff who are able to identify with the need to feel connected and welcomed at school may be more open to taking the extra time to check in on their selected group of students, if only to say good morning or inquire about events in the students' lives.

School leaders can collaborate with Educational Leadership programs and work with pre-service administrators on issues of school climate and social justice. Future administrators need to learn to contextualize learning standards and academics within the context of social justice.

For current administrators who may not have had such learning experience during their own schooling, it is an opportunity for growth. For professors of Educational Leadership, it is necessary to stay current with research in the field of social justice education. Currently, there are very few existing models for college-level programming in this area, but there are valuable suggestions in the research (Agosto et al., 2013; Byrne-Jiménez & Orr, 2013; Hesbol, 2013; Reis & Smith, 2013). For example, a collaborative model of learning could involve Educational Leadership programs partnering with school districts where preservice leaders could gain hands-on experience assisting the school climate committee in developing initiatives within the school.

It is emphasized that a school will not be reformed with simple add-ons via first-order change. If students are taught not to call names simply because they want to avoid punishment or avoid offending someone, they are not learning the truth about structural imbalances that exist within the society in which they live. Although the Dignity Act is a great first step in protecting young people from harassment and cruelty, it is, in itself, another list of rules for students to follow.

A program such as PBIS can also be an important element of school reform, but these programs are not always carried out to the same extent, and with no way to measure them, there is a lot of variability in the programs' effectiveness. It is also important to avoid becoming so focused on behaviors and behavior management that this does not preclude educators from seeing the bigger picture of systematic injustice. School leaders will need to be explicit in their desire for shared responsibility in creating an atmosphere that is pleasant, safe, and conducive to learning.

The school community may not assume that the principal values the input of others, and gaining critical insight in a constructive manner will assist in the stakeholder group cohesion and setting purposeful goals for change. One person cannot change all of the obstacles that are often faced in the lives of teachers and students. However, a united group effort can help make the school environment a safer, healthier, and happier place for everyone.

REFERENCES

Agosto, V., Dias, L. R., Kaiza, N. McHatton, P. A., & Elam, D. (2013). Culture-based leadership and preparation: A qualitative metasynthesis of the literature. In L. C. Tillman & J. J. Scheurich (Eds.). *Handbook of research on educational leadership for equity and diversity.* New York, NY: Routledge.

Birkett, M., Espelage, D. L., & Koenig, B. W. (2009). LGB and questioning students in schools: The moderating effects of homophobic bullying and school climate on negative outcomes. *Journal of Youth and Adolescence, 38*(7), 989–1000.

Blum, R. W. (2005). A case for school connectedness. *Association for Supervision and Curriculum Development, 62*(7), 16–20.

Borman, G., Hewes G., Overman, L., & Brown, S. (2003, Summer). Comprehensive school reform and achievement: A meta-analysis. *Review of Educational Research, 73*(2), 125–230.

Byrne-Jiménez, M., & Orr, M. T. (2013). Evaluating social justice leadership preparation. In L. C. Tillman & J. J. Scheurich (Eds.). *Handbook of research on educational leadership for equity and diversity.* New York, NY: Routledge.

Cohen, J. (2014). School climate policy and practice trends: A paradox. A commentary. Teachers College Record. Retrieved from http://www.tcrecord.org ID Number: 17445

Cohen, J., McCabe, E. M., Michelli, N. M., & Pickeral, T. (2009). School climate: Research, policy, practice, and teacher education. *Teachers College Record, 11*(1), 180–213.

EdChange. (2014). Critical multicultural pavilion awareness activities. Retrieved from http://www.edchange.org/multicultural/activities/inclusion.html

Faster, D., & Lopez, D. (2013). School climate and assessment. In T. Dary & T. Pickeral (Ed.). School climate practices for implementation and sustainability. A school climate practice brief (Vol. 1). New York, NY: National School Climate Center.

Haynes, N., Emmons, C., & Woodruff, D. (1998). School development program effects: Linking implementation to outcomes. *Journal of Education for Students Placed at Risk, 3,* 71–86.

Herrity, V. A., & Glassman, N. S. (2010). Training administrators for culturally and linguistically diverse school populations: Opinions of expert practitioners. *Journal of School Leadership, 20,* 57–76.

Hesbol, K. A. (2013). Preparing leaders to reculture schools as inclusive communities of practice. In L. C. Tillman & J. J. Scheurich (Eds.). *Handbook of research on educational leadership for equity and diversity.* New York, NY: Routledge.

Howard, G. (1999). *We can't teach what we don't know: White teachers, multiracial schools.* New York: Teachers College Press.

Jenlink, P. M., & Jenlink, K. E. (2012). Examining leadership as public policy for social justice. *International Journal of Educational Leadership Preparation, 7*(3), 1–16.

King, J. E. (1991). Dysconscious racism: Ideology, Identity, and the miseducation of teachers. *Journal of Negro Education, 60,* 133–145.

Mullen, C. A. (2011). 21st-century priorities for leadership education and prospective school leaders. *Scholar-Practitioner Quarterly, 4*(4), 331–333.

National School Climate Council. (2007). The school climate challenge: Narrowing the gap between school climate research and school climate policy, practice guidelines and teacher education policy. Retrieved from http://www.schoolclimate.org/publications/policybriefs.php

The New York State Dignity for All Students Act (Dignity Act). (revised 2013). A resource and promising practices guide for school administrators and faculty. Retrieved from http://www.p12.nysed.gov/dignityact/documents/DignityForAllStudentsActGuidance_POSTING.pdf

Osher, D., Spier, E., Kendziora, K., & Cai, C. (2009). Improving academic achievement through improving school climate and student connectedness. Paper presented at the annual meeting of the American Educational Research Association, San Diego, CA. Retrieved from http://alaskaice.org/wordpress/wp-content/uploads/2010/11/090414_AIR_AERA_Improving AcademicAchievement ThroughImprovingSchool ClimateandStudent Connectedness.pdf

Piscatelli, J., & Lee, C. (2011). State policies on school climate and bully prevention efforts: Challenges and opportunities for deepening state policy support for safe and civil schools. National School Climate Center. Retrieved from http://www.schoolclimate.org/climate/documents/policyscan.pdf

Positive Behavioral Interventions and Supports. (2014). Effective discipline for student success. PBIS_factsheet_flier_web.pdf. Retrieved from pbis.org.

Reis, N. M., & Smith, A. (2013). Rethinking the universal approach to the preparation of school leaders. In L. C. Tillman & J. J. Scheurich (Eds.). *Handbook of research on educational leadership for equity and diversity*. New York, NY: Routledge.

Safe Supportive Learning School Climate Measurement. (2014). Retrieved from http://safesupportivelearning.ed.gov/topic-research/school-climate-measurement

Thapa, A., Cohen, J., Higgins-D'Alessandro, A., & Guffey, S. (2012). School climate research summary: August 2012. In *School Climate Brief* (Vol. 3). New York, NY: National School Climate Center.

Chapter Eight

Learning from Teachers

Critically Conscious Educational Leadership for Engaging Diverse Families in Title I Schools

Cherrel Miller Dyce and
Buffie Longmire-Avital

INTRODUCTION

Engaging diverse families and communities in schooling is paramount in order to close the achievement gap, increase the cultural competencies of administrators and teachers, and promote equity and excellence for the academic and social success of children. Empirically, studies (Epstein & Hollifield, 1996; Lim, 2008) confirm the many benefits to children, parents, educators, and schools when families are engaged in education.

Benefits to children include (1) increased achievement despite socio-economic status, race or ethnicity, or parental educational level, (2) parents becoming more sensitive and responsive to schooling, (3) teachers experiencing higher morale when families are involved, and (4) schools gaining a better reputation in the community (Lim, 2008). In this era of accountability, standards and assessments, administrators, teachers, and other educational leaders in Title I and high poverty schools must find meaningful ways to engage diverse families despite the deficit discourse surrounding these communities.

The excuse that families in high poverty schools don't care about their child's education is not valid, neither is it supported by research, and this dominant narrative continues to pathologize low-income, immigrant, and culturally and linguistically diverse communities. As such, educational leadership that dismantles the deficit narrative, raises the critical consciousness of teachers, interrogates the etiology of inequities, and examines the systemic nature of poverty is necessary in order to close the opportunity gap (Milner,

2012) and increase collaboration with diverse families. Similar sentiments are echoed in the literature, and according to Rodriguez and Fabionar (2010):

> Poverty is inextricably linked to population histories and is often experienced, defined, and contested differently along racial, ethnic, and gender lines. The acknowledgement of the systemic nature of poverty and oppression can help leaders to better understand their campus dynamics and the needs of individual learners, align school and community resources with greater efficacy and innovation, and surface and interrupt school policies and practices that reinforce social inequality. (p. 55)

Using narratives and survey data from teachers in one Title I school, this chapter discusses the importance of engagement in Title I schools and how principals and other educational leaders can utilize these teacher narratives to become more efficacious border crossers in order to promote school success for diverse families and children.

Based on the authors' positionality and extensive work in the communities with vulnerable, diverse, and marginalized populations, we use the term family and community engagement instead of parental involvement. Our heuristic experience with diverse families and communities was our rationale for not using the term parental involvement and this is similar to Lightfoot (2004) who contends:

> That the meanings of socially loaded terms such as *parental involvement* are multiple, and they are laden with power implications. Such terms are like portfolios, which have been stuffed with complex, varied, and power-laden meanings. Second, linkages between particular meanings, or metaphors of participation and particular social groups, are not free but rather constrained by habitual association. Finally, because the metaphors and other imagery we use to apply terms such as parental involvement to particular groups are used so habitually that they become invisible, they are difficult to question and difficult to change. (p. 92)

In providing a counternarrative for the culturally sensitive forms of engagement that are needed in Title I schools, we use the term family and community engagement because we understand the political context of language and the power inherent in language as an engine of control and disenfranchisement of certain populations.

Although the term parental involvement will be used sporadically in the chapter when discussing the work of other researchers, family and community engagement is our preferred concept because it:

1. is more culturally sensitive and accommodates various family configurations (kinship and non-kinship) as some children may not have or live with parents;

2. accommodates for the sociocultural factors affecting children outside the classroom;
3. denotes that action is required from all parties, as engagement goes beyond just being involved.

We suggest that educational leaders adopt the aforementioned components of family and community engagement as they are more robust and culturally applicable to the experiences, systems, and types of engagement found in schools with the Title I classification.

The Title I categorization began under the Elementary and Secondary Education Act of 1965 with the provision to provide financial and educational resources to children in high poverty schools (Taylor & Teddlie, 1999). The goal of Title I grants is to help students in poverty reach educational success by providing added resources to close the achievement gap (Office of Planning, Evaluation and Policy Development, U.S. Department of Education, 2011).

According to the National Assessment of Title I Report (2007), the numbers of students receiving Title I funds have tripled increasing from 6.7 million in 1994–1995 to 20 million in 2004–2005. Furthermore, approximately 93 percent of school districts across this country and 56 percent of all public schools receive Title I funds (National Center for Education Evaluation and Regional Assistance, Institute of Education Sciences, U.S. Department of Education, 2007). This report further denotes that a majority of the Title I funds are awarded to mostly elementary schools with roughly 72 percent of the Title I recipients located in kindergarten through the sixth grade. In addition, students of color comprise two-thirds of Title I participants, and Title I funds are often used on instruction, salaries, instructional materials, and enhancing other instructional services and resources.

A central requirement for schools receiving Title I funds is that schools create opportunities to increase parental involvement (Marschall, Shah, & Donato, 2012). Local schools and their district leaders are charged with creating a parent involvement plan to engage families and communities for school success. Thus, family and community engagement in Title I and high poverty schools is not only crucial but also imperative to help bridge the achievement gap for diverse families and students. Below is a chart that can help educational leaders reflect on strength-based perspectives and deficit-based perspectives.

In Title I and high poverty schools, effective school leaders must move beyond the deficit perspective of families and students as lacking capital and radically adopt the position that diverse families possess community cultural wealth (Yosso, 2005) and that school success, growth, and effectiveness are connected broadly to the health and fecundity of the community (Miller, Brown, & Hopson, 2011).

Strengths-based Perspective

You recoginize that difference does not mean deficit.

You seek knowledge of the community by immersing yourself in the community outside the school.

You hold high expectations for all students.

You see families and communities as partners.

You refrain from action and language that renders families powerless.

You reconize that families are the experts on their student.

You use nontraditional forms of strategies to engage families.

You see yourself as a learner and not the authority.

You are able to recognize your own privilege and identity in relation to students and families.

Deficit Perspectices

You are uncomfortable around diverse families and communities.

You view families and communities as helpless, lacking the socical and cultural capital to aid in the growth and development of students.

You are biased, prejudiced and discriminatory against families and communities because of your lack of knowledge.

You have never visited the community surrounding the school but consider yourself an expert in community matters.

You use the students' culture and blame underachievment on cultural factors.

You never examine your identity, race, class, or cultural status.

You don't recognize your own privilege.

Figure 8.1

Such positionality is needed in order to galvanize teachers and other school personnel for successful partnerships and collaborations with diverse families. Freire (1992), in his well-known book *Pedagogy of the Oppressed*, posits a similar perspective in terms of understanding one's positionality, especially when working with oppressed and marginalized populations. Freire labels such positionality development as conscientization, which is the process of fully understanding the role of privilege, power, identity, and culture and how these forces affect personal and institutionalized relationships and settings. Hence, a leader who lacks a critically conscious epistemic stance is undoubtedly a barrier to effective family and community engagement.

Given the research on the lack of experience with diversity that is often experienced in teacher education and educational leadership programs, school leaders hoping to engage with human difference should utilize culturally and critically grounded theories and frameworks to help build capacity for creating a vision for leading their school toward more equitable and socially just family engagement practices.

Educational leaders can also use critical self-reflection as a tool to uncover their positionality and praxis for collaborating with diverse communities and families. Therefore, central to equitable and critically conscious leaderships is the use of critical self-reflection as a conduit for democratic leadership. Mullen, English, and Kealy (2014) declare that "the bedrock of educational leadership is the identity of the leader him or herself" (p. 8). Knowing oneself is the key outcome of critical self-reflection; Davis (2011) terms such reflection as looking inside ourselves.

This personal deconstruction is similar to conscientization, and Mezirow (1998) encourages the use of critical self-reflection as a tool to examine intentions, values, beliefs, and feelings. In fact, Mezirow (1990) forwards that when critical reflection is practiced, it can lead to transformational outcomes. This is essential because a critical analysis of a school leaders' positionality allows him or her to evaluate and antagonize personal biases and prejudices regarding teacher cultural competency, as well as the students, families, and communities who interface with Title I and high poverty schools.

As a result of critical self-reflection, educational leaders are able to position themselves for more culturally competent leadership. According to Hernandez and Kose (2012), cultural competence should be the cornerstone of principal training, preparation, and practice. Intentional reflection can often result in a heightened sense of consciousness and sensitivity by manifesting in leaders' strengths and weaknesses. Terrell and Lindsey (2009) points to the coterminous nature of reflection by school leaders and the intercultural outcome of culturally competent leadership. They state "since we cannot live each other's culture, it becomes imperative that we begin our leadership journey by looking inward to ourselves and understanding our reactions to people who are culturally different from us" (p. 10).

It is this introspection that can become a catalyst for educational leaders to value their own cultural wealth thereby beginning the process of reconstruction, thus seeing themselves as cultural beings and not as cultureless. Hernandez and Kose (2012) forward that culturally competent educational leaders may better prepare students to navigate a multicultural and diverse society. Based on the narratives from teachers in this study, educational leaders may want to consider the following in order to create culturally competent engagements:

- Embrace difference versus tolerating them
- Adopt student and family-centered language
- Be seen greeting families, alongside other educators at key times: in the morning, at dismissal, and school event
- Provide teachers with the flexibility to engage families outside the school walls
- Provide yearlong professional development focus on diversity and family engagement
- Use discretionary funds to create nontraditional family-engagement activities

Most importantly, culturally competent leaders have a vision for hope. They understand that "no change is possible without hope—hope for social justice and transformation" (Pratt-Adams, Maguire, & Burns, 2010, p. 156).

Miller et al. (2011) also suggest the Freirian influenced standpoint that love, hope, and trust should be considered as critical tools for educational leaders in transforming urban education and the complexities, which arise for administrators who work in such context. Overall, equitable, critically conscious, and culturally competent educational leadership is a particular standpoint philosophy that reflects a more humanist pedagogical positioning.

Salazar's (2013) concept of humanizing pedagogy provides educational leaders with the tools to make the paradigmatic shift from deficit perspectives to more liberating paradigms, which view diverse families, students, and their communities as culturally rich meccas overflowing with cultural and social capital that principals and other administrators can empower engagement initiatives. Salazar lists the following as tenets for educators who want to embark on the journey of humanizing pedagogy:

1. The full development of the person is essential for humanization.
2. To deny someone else's humanization is also to deny one's own.
3. The journey for humanization is an individual and collective endeavor toward critical consciousness.
4. Critical reflection and action can transform structures that impede our own and others' humanness, thus facilitating liberation for all.
5. Educators are responsible for promoting a more fully human world through their pedagogical principles and practices.

Leading with equity, social justice, and culture at the forefront will aid educational leaders to more effectively engage families and communities in Title I and high poverty school as such leadership is more transformational in nature and is more culturally synchronized with the cultural practices of diverse students and communities. There is growing research on transformational leadership in schools (Hernandez & Kose, 2012) thus, school leaders who operate from a transformational leadership framework are more relational and place an emphasis on relationship, as well as building and trust (Lynch, 2012), thus engendering a campus environment that is reflective of aspiration, motivation, development, individual concern, and thoughtfulness.

It is in this canonical landscape that educational leaders can learn from the stories gathered from teachers in this study to further their vision for engaging diverse families and communities. Without a critical examination of leadership philosophy and positionality, any plans to engage diverse families in Title I and high poverty schools are bound to fail. Hence, in order to fully and meaningfully engage diverse families and communities in Title I and high poverty schools, educational leaders must first consciously examine their own epistemological, ontological, and axiological frames of reference. Doing so will help to reconcile whether their positionality and philosophical frameworks for engaging families are centered in a strength or deficit perspective.

STUDY CONTEXT

A mixed methods study that was conducted at Trails Elementary School (TES), which is a high poverty Title I school in a small urban school district in the Southern United States. The communities that fall within the school zone are considered working to lower middle class. Parents of children who are employed and generating income have a household that is often classified as just above the poverty line. TES has a population of 580 students, with an average class size of 23 students. The school has a mostly white staff and faculty, many identifying as female.

The administrative staff consists of one principal, one assistant principal, a social worker and school counselor, an academic coach, a nurse, and a psychologist that is shared with another school. Additionally, the student population is about 49 percent black, 31 percent white, and 20 percent Hispanic and other. Approximately 19 percent of the teachers have advanced degrees, and 100 percent of the classes are taught by highly qualified teachers, with 96 percent of the teachers being fully licensed.

Qualitative data was gathered from twelve elementary teachers via a focus group and quantitative data from an anonymous online survey sent to entire school faculty, administrators, and allied staff; nineteen surveys were completed. The survey requested demographic information, teaching experience, and perceptions of the school community cohesiveness. For the focus group data, the faculty was invited to participate in the group at one of their professional development sessions with the first author. During the focus group faculty were asked to discuss multiple topics related to engagement such as describe the perceptions and attitudes toward engaging diverse families as well as define the concept of family and community engagement.

Understanding the dynamic and fluid relationships among families, schools, and communities is essential for fostering academic growth and achievement in students. Although educational leaders are often at the helm of the stewardship of these interconnected relationships, to generate sustained and effective progress, educational leaders must first value the expert knowledge of families and communities.

Olsen and Fuller (2008) position that educators should view families as experts by understanding that "although schools assumed more of the educational responsibilities, families continue to be the first and most important teachers of children because it is through families that children learn how to live in their worlds" (p. 4). Amatea (2013) encourages teachers and other educators to equalize their relationships with families and communities by sharing roles as experts in a nonlinear manner. This allows for diffusion of power and the infusion of collaboration in order to move from the paradigm of "doing to or for families" (Amatea, 2013, p. 10) to "working with and learning from families" (Amatea, 2013, p. 10). Ultimately, this is about building a school community, where the administrators, teachers, supporting staff, and families are all intricately linked together in a common goal for student success in a thriving academic environment.

TEACHER NARRATIVES: WHAT EDUCATIONAL LEADERS CAN LEARN?

Based on our study and narratives from the teachers we studied, three central themes emerged as pedagogies of possibilities that might assist educational leaders in engaging diverse families. They are (1) helping teachers building community within the school and outside community, (2) valuing family and community difference, and (3) allowing curricular freedom for teachers to value home-based capital.

Understanding School as a Community. An examination of the concepts *school* and *community* is crucial in framing how administrators and teachers engage with and create meanings for these constructs. Redding (1991) makes the often overlooked observation that the task of identifying a school as a community is not an easy one. Redding suggests that simply labeling a school as a community ignores that this is only one of three constructs that concurrently exists. For Redding, these constructs are (1) the school *as* the community, (2) the school *in* the community, and (3) the school *and* the community.

This first enmeshed perspective, *the schools as the community*, reflects a very school-centered viewpoint, where nothing outside the school is relevant to developing one's sense of community within the school. An administrator or teacher may hold this perspective if he or she is not a member of the immediate geographic neighborhood that surrounds the school. The main reason for being in this community is to work in the school, and if one is not integrated into the larger neighborhood that feeds the school, it is possible to perceive only the school as the community.

This view of community often contributes to cultural inversion (Ogbu, 1992), which is an "us" versus "them" perspective, where the families representing the "them" are seen as powerless, not capable, and limited partners in education. For others, their perspective might reflect the second concept, *where the school is at the epicenter of the community*, and is symbolically reflective of the larger community. This means for some the school and the community have no boundaries between them. Students in the school may have this perspective.

Consider children who attend the local elementary school. When they arrive at school, they are greeted by other peers whom they have seen in their neighborhood. A child's next-door neighbor could be in the same class, and the children that this child plays with at recess are the same children the child plays with at home during nonschool hours. The interaction or layering of both the school and the community is a viewpoint that is reminiscent of Brofenbrenner's (1979) ecological theory for understanding child development.

According to Brofenbrenner's wildly lauded theory, in order to fully understand child development, people must consider the context the child is developing in. That context is multilayered and includes both people and places. The most immediate contexts (microsystems) for the child are the people and places the child visits and/or interacts with frequently, if not daily; both school and family would be listed in this level.

The working relationship among microsystem constructs creates the contextual space for the mesosystem. The merger of school and community is a primary mesosystem for many school-aged children and their families. According to research, this kind of school is considered a true community school, where both families and the school are interdependent on each other. In this study, the teachers at Trails Elementary were aware that their students blurred the boundaries between school and the residential community. This perspective is more conducive as it provides a nuanced understanding from which to create culturally sensitive and mutually beneficial family engagement plans.

Finally, for others, there is a clear divide *between the community and the school*. The intra- or inter-position of the school and the community (or neighborhood) may be unique to each school and/or neighborhood. When administration and teachers don't move past the formal boundaries of the school, the message sent to parents and extended family members of students is that these are concurrent communities as opposed to an integrated one.

Families are tied to both the school setting and the larger neighborhood. The fact that a student's assigned school is determined primarily by where the student lives may make it hard for students and families to think of school as separate from the community. This is particularly true for Title I schools that cater to low-income families from the surrounding neighborhood and are less likely to house magnet programs that pull students from across the district. However, teachers are not assigned to schools based on their residence. For example, in the case of Trails Elementary, teachers reported an average driving commute to school of 14 miles.

The range of reported distances in our study was from 3 to 40 miles. This means that for most of the teachers at Trails Elementary, they had dual community membership, the community where their primary residence was located and the community of the school. Although the majority of the teachers at Trails Elementary lived outside of the zoned neighborhood for the school, many of the teachers had spent almost their entire career at Trails Elementary or another Title I school. For many the length of time affiliated with the school could create a relationship with the school and/or surrounding neighborhood that could rival a similar relationship with a person both affiliated with the school and living in the local community.

One of the newer teachers at Trails Elementary reinforced the notion of a sense of community developing over time and through investment in the members when she stated:

> I am new to Trails Elementary this year, and for me, I don't necessarily feel like I have become a part of the larger Trails community yet just because I haven't been able to attend some of the community events and visit some of the students' homes, go to the parties and so forth. At my previous school, I was there for three years, and I was able to really invest myself in the families that were there, and I looked forward to doing that at Trails Elementary, but because I just got here, I don't feel like I'm quite there yet. (Title I, Third-Grade Teacher)

Capitalizing on a teacher's extended affiliation as a way to bridge a gap between the community and school is a useful tool for an administrator attempting to increase engagement of families in the school. For example, principals may deliberately pair veteran teachers with new teachers on tasks that involve establishing connections with families. Families that have a history with school will recognize the veteran teacher and may be more willing to engage with the newer teacher as a result of the pairing.

Determining which perspective on school and community an educator, administrator, and families hold is critical to the navigation of relationships and preservation of community inclusiveness. Perhaps the first step in identifying and reflecting on school community perspectives is to examine the perception of community from a deconstructed point of view. Moos' (1973) model for social climate or "sense of community" gives a blueprint for this deconstruction. Social climate and the resulting community can be broken down into three components: relationships, personal development, and system maintenance and change.

Educational leaders can begin this evaluation process by asking all members of the school (i.e., teachers and staff) the following questions to determine the predominate perspective on community: (1) Can you identify any members of your teaching and support staff that have relationships with people other than their students? Specifically, what relationships do they have with key stakeholders in the surrounding neighborhood—such as the families who are the adult residents of the community? What is the collective level of comfort in reaching out to families and the perception of how comfortable they are reaching out to members of the school community, including me, in an administrative role? (2) A primary function of school is the fostering of student personal development, but teacher development is also important. School leaders should determine if teachers feel the school provides them an opportunity to develop, and how do their interactions with families assist in this development, if at all? (3) What are the current expectations regarding your own participation in the school and immediate environment outside the school? Does your school culture encourage innovative approaches to connecting to the larger community? Are there distinct boundaries in regard to school policies and action items that both families and staff adhere to?

Reflecting on these questions may help education leaders identify not only the school climate but also which of Redding's (1991) school community constellations describe their perception of their current environment.

Valuing Family and Community Differences. From our study, participants expressed that teachers must first value the indigenous knowledge of families and communities in order to create engagement pathways that will be participatory, emancipatory, and accessible. As stated by a teacher in this study:

> I think part of it, too, is that most of the faculty here don't deal with Title I issues at home every day. We are not living that lifestyle, and I think it could be very intimidating when you know that you have very little, you may be or not be really well educated, and your job isn't as good. That would be intimidating for me, and I think it is definitely up to us [teachers] to make a huge effort from day one to make sure that they feel that we love them where they are and that they see that. (Title I, Kindergarten Teacher)

For this teacher, her positionality and philosophy of education were evident in that philosophically, she values engagement and connection with families from her first encounter with them, making her critically aware of her own privileges and power in relation to the families in the community.

This sentiment was echoed by many teachers in the focus group who had a keen awareness of "first impressions" and cultural differences. One teacher stated that "I think there are a lot of times when parents come in, and we are little intimidating to them and, there are some things within cultures that I try to be aware of." One example,

> I'm very tall and I know in some cultures that you don't really see this, so I try to not loom over them [families]. I try to sit down and make them feel really comfortable and let them know that it was real, that I'm real, and they can come to me and that their child is so important, you are just making them feel comfortable.

Educational leaders should help teachers and other school administrators further understand families and communities, by providing learning opportunities to help teachers make the paradigmatic shift to not pathologize and relegate families into the binary quadrants of normality versus abnormality with comments such as "my family is normal" or "I come from a family with traditional views," all phrases we have heard from teachers.

A lack of critical consciousness about families and communities automatically cripples the exchange of information, communication, and goodwill across the engagement bridge. If opportunities are not created by the school administrator to allow teachers to examine where they are from and how this is similar or different from the families and students they are trying to engage, then instead of being efficacious border crossers, teachers become reluctant in engaging families, and diverse families are left misunderstood and isolated.

We suggest educational leaders use the following activities to help build competency in this area:

• Year-long professional development on a family and community engagement
• "Where I'm From" poems
• Critical reflection journals
• Staff and grade-level meeting as learning opportunities to help to value community differences

Allowing Curricular Freedom for Teachers to Value Home-Based Capital. Moll, Amanti, Neff, and Gonzalez's (1992) seminal research on funds of knowledge is one methodology to help teachers understand families and communities. Their premise is that by understanding the households of families from strengths and asset-based perspectives, teachers are more likely to glean more holistic cultural knowledge, which will provide relevance for students and families.

According to Moll et al. (1992), funds of knowledge are the "historically accumulated and culturally developed bodies of knowledge and skills essential for household or individual functioning and well-being" (p. 133). The bridge to engagement is more likely to be built when families' voices are more accepted in the classroom and where families are seen as experts. This quote from one of the teachers exemplifies this best:

> You know your class and that their cultural background forbade anything with Halloween. I didn't even do fun things with cute little witches or bats or things like that. If I was teaching a theme, our fall or other celebrations would be done differently. We spoke about the day of the dead instead of just focusing on Halloween. Again that was something that I knew about my class and something that you know about your individual class, and you do that a little bit without realizing. You teach your kids, but you know your makeup, and you know what's appropriate or what's not appropriate for your class. (Title I, Specialist)

In this example, the teacher moved beyond the traditional Western celebration of Halloween and included more culturally relevant discussions about the Day of the Dead, which allows students to connect with cultural practices of which Trails Elementary has a significant student population.

Educational leaders should encourage teachers to assign home-based assignments where students see themselves as experts in reporting to the classroom their family and community traditions, ways of knowing and being, as this is central to understanding families and communities, since the student is the teacher's central point of contact to the community on a daily basis.

So, providing teachers with the curricular incentive and freedom to create a math project that requires students to use a favorite family recipe will gain valuable information, while at the same time connecting to state standards. Additionally, a language arts lesson can be the beginnings of a targeted family engagement plan if educational leaders provide the necessary resources for teachers to give their students audio recorders and ask them to interview a family member or someone in the community about his or her life. The second part of the assignment would require students to create their own biographies, allowing the students to represent themselves in a culturally connected manner.

Administrators who are not married to the curriculum must make it a priority to engage teachers in understanding the funds of knowledge that students and their families possess in order to make teaching, learning, and family and community engagement more successful. The relevancy of the curriculum is essential when trying to engage diverse families and communities.

Culturally aligned curricular activities allow for less threatening, nontraditional forms of home-based family engagement, which are more culturally appropriate when working with the various types of diversities found in Title I and high poverty schools. Such relevancy can only increase a campus climate where the consanguinity between home and school is welcome, celebrated, and cherished.

Since Title I schools are mandated to have family engagement plans, understanding the link between in-school and out-of-school connection is necessary for the implementation of a school's plan to successfully engage families and communities. We suggest that educational leaders utilize the Gonzalez-Mena (2013) approach, which encourages teachers and administrators and schools to adopt a family-centered approach to engagement as this allows for engagement plans that will more directly center the child and family's experiences as one continuous circle, instead of just looking at the needs of the child without considering the context of the family. Understanding family engagement through a family-centered approach promotes collaboration, mutuality, and partnerships where families are seen as inseparable and central to school success (Gonzalez-Mena, 2013).

Strageties for Engagement	Theories for Understanding Families
Seek out professional development in the area of family and community engagement.	BioEcologocial System Theory-Urie Bronfrenbrenner
Attend community functions and seek out community gatekeepers, such as faith based leaders and nonprofit leaders to gain family and community knowledge.	Family Systems Theory–Murray Bowen
Conduct home visits, going as a team with the social worker and counselor.	Sociocultural Theory–Lev Vygotsky
Hold parent teacher conferences at the local library or other facilities.	Ecologies of Parental Engagement in
Visit the community surrounding the school frequently.	Urban Education–Angela Calabrese Barton et al.
Utilize the school's social worker and counselor in helping you build capital with parents	

Figure 8.2

Schools receiving Title I funds are charged with creating an effective Title I family engagement plan in order to comply with their Title I grant (Epstein, 2010). Administrators who are in charge of the day-to-day operation of the school and the Title I budget must rely on teachers to help facilitate a successful family engagement plan. The conundrum is, however aspirational these engagement plans, if they are not culturally specific to the students, families, and communities surrounding the school, then partial or full engagement will not be actualized.

Educational leaders must be keenly aware that often teachers become frustrated at the lack of engagement of the students' families despite the many notices sent home, the phone calls, and the importance of the event at the school. In Xiong and Obiakor's (2013) study of non-Hmong principals and Hmong parents, they concur that, when the backgrounds of administrators are different from the parent or family constituents, the possibility of cultural misunderstanding is increased, and this can lead to poor or a lack of communication between home and school (Xiong & Obiakor, 2013).

In other words, aspirational engagement from teachers and administrators is not enough, as true or actualized engagement must consider outside school forces as central pillars of any engagement strategy or plan, essentially adopting Redding's (1991) view of the school in the community. At the Title I school, in which this study was conducted, many of the teachers in our focus group had a high disposition for aspirational engagement. However, this was often not actualized because the forms of engagement strategies utilized were mostly traditional in-school forms of engagement, such as parent-teacher meetings, book fairs, and other events that required the parents to come to school.

In creating a plan of action for diverse family engagement, educational leaders should help teachers move from aspirational engagement, which is having the aptitude for engagement but not using culturally effective tools to actualized engagement. Administrators and other leaders can employ Gestwicki's (2013) recommendation to help teachers understand the demographics of families today and why an understanding of these factors is paramount when creating realistic family engagement plans. These demographical factors are (1) marital instability and the increase in unmarried mothers, (2) changes in role behavior, (3) mobility, urbanization, and economic conditions, (4) decreasing family size, (5) increased rate of social change, (6) development of a child-centered society, and (7) stress in modern living (Gestwicki, 2013).

Couchenour and Chrisman (2013) broaden these factors with helping teachers understand race, ethnicity, culture, language, economic differences, and geographic regions. A considering of these factors will help teachers like the ones in this study who have a high degree of critical awareness of culture, identity, and educational outcomes but need to look outside the school walls in creating more culturally sensitive forms of engagement.

WHAT ARE CONTEXTUALLY RELEVANT FORMS OF ENGAGEMENT?

A new afterschool tutoring and activities program was starting in the community room within a public housing complex. One week prior to the start of the program, flyers were posted all over the neighborhood and inside buildings. Families walking around were approached and invited to send their school-aged children. For the first day of the program, a fleet of volunteers arrived ready to work with dozens of children, but no one from the community came.

For thirty disappointing minutes, the volunteers and their director sat in the room waiting on the arrival of children. At the thirty-minute mark, the director told her volunteers to continue waiting; she was going to go door-to-door. Weaving through the apartment complex and its narrow paths, the director knocked on doors that she knew had school-aged children. The director led a parade of children with homework back to the community room. The door-to-door approach was done for another week, and by the third week, excited parents were walking over their eager children. As a community psychologist and director of that program in a low-income urban city in Pennsylvania, this was my first experience with nontraditional forms of engagement.

The director was thrilled that parents had become engaged in the program and were bringing their children on their own. Curious about the transformation from hesitant to fully invested, the director asked a few of the parents what made them change their minds. They told her they felt she was serious about being here and that not being afraid to come to their door showed how committed she was to this program and helping them. The director had earned their trust.

As an outsider or nonresidential member of the community, a teacher can't foster engagement from families without earning their trust (LaRocque, Kleiman, & Darling, 2011). In the example of the afterschool director, trust was earned by going door-to-door to recruit children and their families. The parents of the children were aware of the program; they had seen the flyers but were skeptical to send their children because they had not made a personal connection with the program.

Often, teachers reach out to parents and families through phone calls, emails, and letters home. However, for many families, this approach is seen as distant and not a valid facilitator of true relationship building. For diverse families, the path to sustained engagement may look more like this:

> One year when we were doing fall and spring musicals, one of my parents called and said, "I don't have a car. My car is broken down, and I can't bring my kid to the musical tonight. Can you pick my kid up?" And, I said sure and I drove to an area that is one of our more deprived areas, satellite areas.... All the kids playing in the street saw me. They were so excited; they all want to get in my car, and I drove eight kids here [school] so they could be in the play. They all went home and told their parents.... Those moms and dads came in the spring, they found cars, their kid was happy, and they were happy in school. It was one kid, then it turned into six kids, and by the spring we had more kids, so I think it's a slow thing, but it can happen one kid at a time ... small group engagement that is going to turn into a large engagement, and it will spread. I think it is definitely doable. (Title I, Second-Grade Teacher)

This teacher's facilitation of family engagement was ignited by her willingness to help a stranded family. Many families face challenges that impede their ability to engage in school programming, which can be reflective of families' economic need at Title I schools. She also broke down the barrier between school and community.

She came to the students' neighborhood, much like the afterschool director knocked on apartment doors. Again, the challenge for many Title I schools is that they are staffed by teachers who are not residents of the immediate neighborhood. Students see their teachers in the classroom or on school grounds, and that is it. Creating opportunities to connect with students and families in their community is critical to the sustained engagement of families (Barton, Drake, Perez, Louis, & George, 2004).

Not all teachers are in a position to offer rides to and/or from school to student homes. However, showing support of the community that feeds the school's population can be done by going to out-of-school events in the local community. Open houses at schools are considered an opportunity to meet with families, but it still means the family must come to you, the teacher. What would happen if you brought the school to them? An innovative educational leader should consider organizing a meet-and-greet session at local community spots, such as a resource center or community religious space, for teachers, students, and families.

If students are involved in extracurricular activities, such as dance or sports, encouraging teachers to attend as a spectator could help parents feel more comfortable with them as well. Remember, as the nonresident community members, the divide between the school and the surrounding community might be very visible to you and your staff. However, that divide may not exist for students and family. A teacher's ability and willingness to move beyond the classroom space to the larger community may further the teacher's attempts to build trust and community building (Beckett, Glass, & Moreno, 2013). When working with diverse families, educational leaders need to guide their teachers in the use of a flipped model of engagement.

In a flipped engagement model, traditional community and engagement is not avoided, but it is used less. Instead, teachers break through the barriers between residential community space and school space often. One teacher felt that, by actively moving between the residential space and the school space, the students' belief that the two spaces were integrated would develop. She said, "I think also when they see us in other places than just school, they need to see that we are the same people and have the same emotions and caring for them at Wal-Mart that we do here 'Am I going to get my hug?' 'Am I going to … whatever that kind of thing is. Is she going to care about me different[ly] somewhere else,' so yeah, I think that makes a community all over the place."

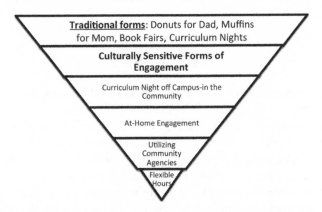

Figure 8.3

In this teacher's experience, reaching out to students in nonschool spaces helped the students feel more present in the school community. This outreach to students will also foster the relationship building with their families. Families may feel more comfortable approaching a teacher in nonschool settings. These informal meetings could serve as potential gateways to ongoing dialogue with the parents. Families will be more willing to engage if they believe the teacher is genuinely invested in their child and their child's experiences (De Carvalho, 2014).

Putting the model of flipped engagement into action is not easy. Here are some things to encourage your teachers to think about: What is the ratio between notes/emails or calls home to face-to-face encounters? A letter home or phone calls are still reasonable ways to engage families, but if the only time teachers are seeing parents is at conferences, then they have not broken through the barrier between school and community.

If you are not familiar with the neighborhood, consider picking up a local newspaper or newsletter to find out what is going on. Incorporate the announcement of upcoming local events into your presentations and meetings with teaching staff. Even ask yourself, how many nonschool community events could I attend in any given term? What about attending a religious service? If you have gone to a community event to support the students (e.g., a children's sporting event), how many families did you speak to while there? If there are teachers or other staff members who have an already strong relationship with families and the larger community at school, have you sat down and talked to them? Would you be willing to go with them to an event? Again, sometimes being seen with an insider will create an opportunity for you to gain access to a community.

Finally, have you walked around the school neighborhood yet and have you encouraged your teachers to do the same? Being visible and showing students and families that everyone is in this together is critical for engaging all families.

CONCLUSION

First, this chapter began with the history of Title I schools and the families they serve.

Second, we asked you to examine your philosophy and positionality of education because, as a teacher educator and community psychologist, we believe that understanding your positionality within a strengths-based perspective is foundational for your critical work with families.

Third, we encouraged you to critically reflect how your understanding of families is by disassociating yourself from the binary constraints of normality versus abnormality classifications for families.

Fourth was an understanding of the school as a community and the challenges of being a dual citizen in both the school community and your residential community.

Fifth, we further examined that having good intentions may not be synonymous with culturally sensitive forms of engagement, so we suggest that the metamorphosis to actualized engagement practices will again test your skills in critical self-reflection.

Finally, we suggest that, although your primary context in education will remain the classroom, authentic family engagement requires moving past the physical space of the classroom using our model of flipped engagement.

REFERENCES

Amatea, E. (2013). *Building culturally responsive family-school.* Upper Saddle River, NJ: Pearson Merrill Prentice Hall.

Barton, A. C., Drake, C., Perez, J. G., Louis, K. S., & George, M. (2004). Ecologies of parental engagement in urban education. *Educational Researcher, 33*(4), 3–12.

Beckett, L., Glass, R. D., & Moreno, A. P. (2013). A pedagogy of community building: Re-imagining parent involvement and community organizing in popular education efforts. *Association of Mexican American Educators Journal, 6*(1), 5–14.

Brofenbrenner, U. (1979). *The ecology of human development: Experiments by nature and design.* Cambridge, MA: Harvard University Press.

Couchenour, D., & Chrisman, K. (2013). *Families, schools and communities: Together for young children.* Belmont, CA: Cengage Learning.

Davis, B. M. (2011). Respect. In A. M. Blankstein & P. D. Houston (Eds.), *Leadership for social justice and democracy in our schools* (Vol. 9, pp. 1–23). Thousand Oaks, CA: Corwin Press.

De Carvalho, M. E. (2014). *Rethinking family-school relations: A critique of parental involvement in schooling.* New York, NY: Psychology Press.

Epstein, J. L. (2010). School/family/community partnerships: Caring for the children we share. *Phi Delta Kappan, 92*(3), 81–96.

Epstein, J. L., & Hollifield, J. H. (1996). Title I and school–family–community partnerships: Using research to realize the potential. *Journal of Education for Students Placed at Risk, 1*(3), 263–278.

Freire, P. (1992). *Pedagogy of the oppressed.* New York, NY: Continuum Press.

Gestwicki, C. (2013). *Home, school, and community relations.* Belmont, CA: Cengage Learning.

Gonzalez-Mena, J. (2013). *Foundations of early childhood education: Teaching children in a diverse society.* Upper Saddle River, NJ: McGraw-Hill Higher Education.

Hernandez, F., & Kose, B. W. (2012). The developmental model of intercultural sensitivity: A tool for understanding principals' cultural competence. *Education and Urban Society, 44*(4), 512–530.

LaRocque, M., Kleiman, I., & Darling, S. M. (2011). Parental involvement: The missing link in school achievement. *Preventing School Failure, 55*(3), 115–122.

Lightfoot, D. (2004). "Some parents just don't care": Decoding the meanings of parental involvement in urban schools. *Urban Education, 39*(1), 91–107.

Lim, S. Y. (2008). Parental involvement in education. In G. Olsen & M. L. Fuller (Eds.), *Home-School Relations* (pp. 127–150). Boston, MA: Allyn & Bacon.

Lynch, M. (2012). *A guide to effective school leadership theories.* Florence, KY: Routledge, Taylor & Francis Group.

Marschall, M. J., Shah, P. R., & Donato, K. (2012). Parent involvement policy in established and new immigrant destinations*. *Social Science Quarterly, 93*(1), 130–151.

Mezirow, J. (1990). How critical reflection triggers transformative learning. *Fostering Critical Reflection in Adulthood,* 1–20.

Mezirow, J. (1998). On critical reflection. *Adult Education Quarterly, 48*(3), 185–198.

Miller, P. M., Brown, T., & Hopson, R. (2011). Centering love, hope, and trust in the community transformative urban leadership informed by Paulo Freire. *Urban Education, 46*(5), 1078–1099.

Milner, H. R. (2012). Beyond a test score: Explaining opportunity gaps in educational practice. *Journal of Black Studies, 43*(6), 693–718.

Moll, L. C., Amanti, C., Neff, D., & Gonzalez, N. (1992). Funds of knowledge for teaching: Using a qualitative approach to connect homes and classrooms. *Theory into Practice, 31*(2), 132–141.

Moos, R. H. (1973). Conceptualization of human environments. *American Psychologist, 28,* 652–665.

Mullen, C. A., English, F. W., & Kealy, W. A. (2014). *The leadership identity journey: An artful reflection.* Lanham, MD: Rowman & Littlefield.

National Center for Education Evaluation and Regional Assistance, Institute of Education Sciences, U.S. Department of Education. (2007). *Final report on the national assessment of Title I: Summary of key findings.* Washington, DC: Author.

Office of Planning, Evaluation and Policy Development, U.S. Department of Education. (2011). The potential impact of revising the Title I comparability requirement to focus on school-level expenditures. A policy brief from the U.S. Department of Education, Policy and Program Studies Service, Alexandria, VA. Retrieved from http://www2.ed.gov/rschstat/eval/title-i/comparability-requirement/comparability-policy-brief.pdf

Ogbu, J. U. (1992). Understanding cultural diversity and learning. *Educational Researcher, 21*(8), 5–14.

Olsen, G. W., & Fuller, M. L. (2008). An introduction to families. In G. W. Olsen & M. L. Fuller (Eds.), *Home school relations: Working successfully with parents and families* (pp. 4–12). Boston, MA: Allyn & Bacon.

Pratt-Adams, S., Maguire, M., & Burns, E. (2010). *Changing urban education.* London, England: Continuum International.

Redding, S. (1991). What is a school community, anyway? *The School Community Journal, 1*(2), 7–9.

Rodriguez, G. M., & Fabionar, J. O. (2010). The impact of poverty on students and schools: Exploring the social justice leadership implications. In C. Marshall & M. Oliva (Eds.), *Leadership for social justice: Making revolutions in education* (pp. 55–73). Boston, MA: Pearson Education/Allyn & Bacon.

Salazar, M. C. (2013). A humanizing pedagogy: Reinventing the principles and practice of education as a journey toward liberation. *Review of Research in Education, 37*(1), 121–148.

Taylor, D. L., & Teddlie, C. (1999). Implementation fidelity in Title I schoolwide programs. *Journal of Education for Students Placed at Risk, 4*(3), 299–319.

Terrell, R. D., & Lindsey, R. B. (2009). *Culturally proficient leadership: The personal journey begins within.* Thousand Oaks, CA: Corwin Press.

Xiong, T. T., & Obiakor, F. E. (2013). Cultural connections and disconnections between non Hmong principals and Hmong parents. *Multicultural Perspectives, 15*(1), 39–45.

Yosso, T. J. (2005). Whose culture has capital? A critical race theory discussion of community cultural wealth. *Race Ethnicity and Education, 8*(1), 69–91.

Index

Academically or Intellectually Gifted
  (AIG) coordinator, 11
administration preparation programs, 75
Allen, R. L., 64
Allen-Collinson, J., 25
Allport, G. W., 79
Amanti, C., 138
Amatea, E., 133
American Psychological Association
  Zero Tolerance Task Force, 44
Applied Research, 8
Atkinson, R., 25
attendance policy, 104–107
autoethnography, 23, 24–26, 34, 37

Baldwin, J., 1
Banks, J., 95
Banks, J. A., 104
Beachum, F., 27
Blackmore, J., 2, 14
Brofenbrenner, U., 135
Bryan M. D., 28, 29
Bryk, A. S., 52
bullying prevention policy, 107–110

change theory, 49–52
Cho, H., 34
Chrisman, K., 141

Circle in the Square: Building
  Community and Repairing Harm in
  School (Riestenberg), 48
Civil Rights Act, 1
class demographics, 10–12
classism, 4
CLD. see culturally and linguistically
  diverse
Coates, L., 101
Codrington, J., 31
community and professional
  environments, 14–16
complacent satisfaction, 1
Conflict Resolution in Education, 54
contextually relevant forms, 141–144
Couchenour, D., 141
critical multicultural approaches, 111
Critical Race Theory (CRT), 65, 73, 100
Critical Race Theory and Racial Identity
  Development, 73
cultural relevance, 94
culturally and linguistically diverse
  (CLD), 99–100
culturally responsive leadership, 26–28
culture change, 57, 58

Dantley, M., 75
Davis, D. M., 27, 130

DeCuir, J. T., 65
democracy, 18
Department of Education (DOE), 49
Department of Educational
    Leadership, 3
Dignity for All Students Act, 115
Dignity for All Students Act
    (DASA), 115
diverse cultural groups, 93–94
Dixon, A. D., 65
doctorate program, 9
Dominguez, R., 7
Duarte, F., 29
Dyson, M., 36, 37

Education Act, 35
education policy, 58
educational administration, 8
educational leaders:
    conscious and skilled actors, 2;
    demand for, 1;
    traditional preparation of, 3
educational leadership, 4
Elementary and Secondary Education
    Act, 129
*Elementary and Secondary Education
    Act* (ESEA), 103
Ellis, C., 26
Ellis, S. N., 33
empowerment, 49–52
English, F. W., 130
English Language Learners
    (ELLs), 16
Epstein, J. L., 101
equity in education, 100
equity teams assess school
    climate, 86–88
ESEA. *see Elementary and Secondary
    Education Act*

Fabionar, J. O., 128
Fairchild, H. H., 31
family engagement, 100–102
Foster, W. F., 27
Frankenberg, R., 65

Freire, P., 130
Fuller, M. L., 133

Gay, G., 23
Gestwicki, C., 141
gifted and talented (GT) programs, 108
Gonzalez- Mena, J., 139
Gonzalez, N., 138
Grover, B. K., 66
Guba, E., 25

Helms, J., 82
Hernandez, F., 131
Hesbol, K. A., 118
Hockey, J., 25
home visits, 91–92
Hopkins, B., 46, 47, 50
Howard, 103, 112
humanities, 4

immigrant population, 128
immigrant populations, 102
immigrant school administrator, 125
immigrant students, 31
Implicit Association Test (IAT),
    80, 81, 82
in-school suspension (ISS) program, 55
Intergroup Contact Hypothesis
    (Allport), 79
International Institute for Restorative
    Practices (IIRP), 54

Jean- Marie, G., 27

Kealy, W. A., 130
Kose, B. W., 131

Ladson- Billings, G., 100
leadership, 49–52
leadership for diversity, 6–7
leadership practices, 5, 28, 31, 35, 37
leadership preparation, 2
leadership theory, 8, 63, 64, 74,
    75, 76, 78
Leadership Theory, 8

liberalism, critique of, 65
Lightfoot, D., 128
Lincoln, Y., 25
Lindsey, R. B., 131
Linton, C., 77

Mahamed, F., 31
McClellan, R., 7
McIntosh, P., 91
McIntyre, 64
McKenzie, K. B., 103
meritocracy, 18
Mezirow, J., 5, 131
minority groups, 79, 84, 86, 87
Moll, L. C., 101, 138
Morrison, B., 45
Mullen, C. A., 130
multicultural education, 79, 90, 100
multiculturalism, 90

National Assessment of Title I
    Report, 129
Neff, D., 138
Nieto, Sonia, 90
No Child Left Behind Act, 103
Noel, J., 80
Normore, A. H., 27

Obiakor, F. E., 140
Office of Civil Rights (OCR), 49
Olsen, G. W., 133
Organizational Development, 8

Pedagogy of the Oppressed (Freire), 130
Pelias, R. J., 25
Perry, P., 65
Pitts, Leonard, 1

Quantz, R. A., 75

racial advisors, role of, 66–76
racial identity, 65, 73, 74, 80, 82–84
racial identity development (RID),
    80–81, 82–84
racism, 4, 34, 35, 64, 65, 66, 67

Redding, S., 134, 137, 140
Reimer, K., 53
relational pedagogies, 46, 47, 48, 54
restorative justice in education (RJE),
    43, 45–48
Riestenberg, N., 48
Rist, R. C., 110
Rodriguez, G. M., 128
Rogers, J., 75

Safe Schools Act, 28, 29
Sagor, S., 33
Salazar, M. C., 132
Salinas, K. C., 101
Sanders, M. G., 101
Scheurich, J. J., 103
school administration, 7, 8
school administrator, 26, 28, 29, 31
school board policy, 28
school climate, 52, 55, 57, 80, 81,
    85, 86–88;
    administrator preparation programs,
    119–120;
    and connectedness, 116;
    Dignity for All Students Act,
    117–119;
    measuring school climate, 122;
    national school climate reform,
    116–117;
    positive school climate, 120–122
school culture, 2, 43, 45, 46, 49, 50,
    52, 53, 57
school discipline, 45, 49, 56, 58
school discipline policies, 49, 56
school environments, 27, 35, 44,
    45, 47, 55
school leaders, 2
school leadership, social change, 3–4
school reform, 49, 50, 51, 53, 54, 55
schools and school policy, 44, 64, 66,
    99, 100, 102–104
schoolwide restorative approaches
    (SWRAs), 47
schoolwide restorative justice, 50–52
secondary school, 28–35

SEL. *see* Social Emotional Learning
sexism, 4
sexual orientation, 4
shades of grey, 12–14
Shields, C., 74, 75
Simon, B. S., 101
Singleton, G., 77
social and multicultural foundations, 4
social change, school leadership for, 3–4
Social Emotional Learning
        (SEL), 47, 48
social foundations, 4–7
Social Foundations of Education, 8
social justice, 2, 3
Social Justice (Nieto, Sonia), 90
social sciences, 4
societal injustices, 74
staff development activities, 88–89
study context, 133–134

Tate, W. F., 100
Tatum, B. D., 82
teacher narratives, 134–141
teaching tolerance, 90–91
Terrell, R. D., 131

Thandeka, 74
Trails Elementary School (TES), 133
transformational learning, 5–6
transformative leadership, 63,
        74, 75, 76
transformative school leaders, 80–85,
        89, 91;
    self-assessment, 80–85;
    staff attitudes, 85–86

Ueland, B., 57
unearned privilege, 91
unlearning biases, 92–93

Viadero, D., 102

*Why Are All the Black Kids Sitting
        Together in the Cafeteria*
        (Tatum), 90

Xiong, T. T., 140

zero tolerance, 44–45
zero tolerance policies, 44, 45, 49,
        50, 56

About the Editors

Ashraf Esmail serves as the Proposal Review Lead and serves on the Publication Committee for the National Association for Multicultural Education. He is the senior editor for the *Journal of Education and Social Justice* and the *International Journal of Leadership, Education, and Business Studies*.

Abul Pitre is professor of educational leadership at Prairie View A&M University, where he teaches courses in multicultural education and leadership. He was appointed Edinboro University's first named professor for his outstanding work in African American education and held the distinguished title of the Carter G. Woodson Professor of Education.

Antonette Aragon is an associate professor in the School of Education and the Center for Educator Preparation at Colorado State University. Utilizing feminist theory, critical race theory, LatCrit, culturally responsive teaching, and social justice emphasizing understandings of self, systemic inequities, and cultural awareness, her scholarship is located at the intersections of social justice equity, educational policy and leadership, technology, and cultural relevant education. She has articles in journals including *Urban Education, Multicultural Education & Technology, Teaching Education, Multicultural Teaching and Learning*, and *Journal of Hispanic Higher Education*.

About the Contributors

Buffie Longmire-Avital is a community psychologist with a public health focus and background in developmental psychology; she is currently an assistant professor of psychology at Elon University, Elon, North Carolina. Broadly, her research interests focus on how psychosocial, cultural, and structural factors contribute to health and educational disparities impacting minority communities. Dr. Longmire-Avital is also a statistical methodologist with an expertise in multivariate regression modeling and mixed-method designs.

Dr. Martha A. Brown is a renowned author, consultant, presenter, researcher, teacher and advocate of restorative justice. She earned her doctorate in Curriculum & Instruction from Florida Atlantic University after exploring restorative schools in the United Kingdom and ultimately conducting her dissertation research in partnership with the Oakland Unified School District in California. Dr. Brown is the Lead Instructor for Simon Fraser University's Continuing Studies Restorative Justice Certificate Program, where she facilitates learning for adult students in Canada, United States, Australia, Africa, and other countries worldwide. She has published several peer reviewed articles, book chapters, and book reviews regarding restorative justice, correctional education, and evaluating art education programs. Dr. Brown has also presented nationally at conferences sponsored by the National Association of Community and Restorative Justice (NACRJ) and the International Conference on Conflict Resolution in Education (CRE). In 2016, Dr. Brown founded RJAE Consulting, Intl. to provide planning, evaluation, and other consulting services to schools, school districts, correctional facilities, and organizations focusing on restorative justice (RJ) or art education (AE). She can be reached at martha@rjaeconsulting.com or through her website, www.rjaeconsulting.com.

Susan Catapano is chair and professor international coordinator holding a doctorate in higher education with concentrations in adult learning and early childhood education. She teaches both undergraduate and graduate courses in curriculum, instruction, and supervision. Her research focus is supporting the development of cultural competence in beginning teachers and school administrators working with diverse learners.

Bryan M. Davis is the superintendent of schools for the Columbus School District in Columbus, Wisconsin. His research interests include urban education and the influence of race on school environments. He completed his dissertation, titled "A Case Study of How White High School Administrators Make Meaning of Their Whiteness," in 2011 at the University of Wisconsin-Milwaukee. His academic writing with the Midwest Critical Whiteness Collective focuses on how school administrators can improve leadership through developing a critical perspective of race in their school environments. He was a contributing author for "McIntosh as Synechdoche: How Teacher Education's Focus on White Privilege Undermines Antiracism" in the Harvard Educational Review in fall of 2013. Davis was nominated for the 2014 Wisconsin Superintendent of the Year Award.

Susan Dodd holds a doctorate in educational psychology and educational administration. She has twelve years of experience working in a public school setting and currently teaches in a collaborative education department where future teachers, counselors, and administrators learn together. Susan's research interests are on issues of school climate and social justice within schools. She works with current and preservice educators on examining issues of inequity within schools.

Cherrel Miller Dyce is an assistant professor of education and faculty fellow at the Center for Race, Ethnicity and Diversity Education at Elon University, Elon, North Carolina. Her research agenda includes issues related to diversity studies, social justice, educational inequities, precollege preparation of students of color, family and community involvement in education, student development, counseling, and mentoring.

Katherine R. Evans is an assistant professor of education at Eastern Mennonite University, teaching courses in special education and educational theory. With a PhD in educational psychology and research from the University of Tennessee in Knoxville, her research, teaching, and scholarship focus on ways in which teachers participate in creating more just and equitable educational opportunities for all students, including those with disability labels, those who exhibit challenging behavior, and those who are marginalized for a variety of reasons, including race, ethnicity, language, sexual orientation, and gender identity. She has published several articles and book chapters related to zero tolerance policies, restorative justice, and school discipline practices, focusing on the ways in which restorative justice are applied to educational contexts.

Dr. Ann E. Lopez is a faculty member in the Department of Leadership, Higher and Adult Education at the Ontario Institute for Studies in Education, University of Toronto. Born and raised in Jamaica she completed her undergraduate studies at the University of the West Indies. She completed her Masters of Education at Brock University and later earned her PhD in curriculum studies at the University of Toronto. Her research and teaching focus on equity and diversity in schooling, culturally responsive teaching approaches that challenge all forms of exclusion, and culturally responsive and socially just leadership. She currently serves as a board member of the National Association of Multicultural Education (NAME) and is the Regional Director for Region 8. Her most recent publication is entitled *Reconceptualizing Teacher Leadership Through Curriculum Inquiry in Pursuit of Social Justice in the International Handbook of Educational Leadership and Social (In) Justice*. A former secondary school teacher and school administrator she is committed to ensuring that all students, particularly those who have been traditionally underserved, are included and engaged in their learning environments and fully prepared to be productive citizens in an increasingly globalized world.

María L. Gabriel has worked as a PK–12 Latina educator in public education since 1997, working with culturally and linguistically diverse communities and their educators. She has a focus on increasing access and opportunity for students through engaging families, professional development, and direct student support. Her research interests include Latin@ student achievement, culturally responsive pedagogy, and educational equity. Her work has been published in journals such as Cuaderno de Investigación en la Educación, Educational Leadership, and the Journal of Latinos and Education.

Michelle Yvonne Szpara is currently serving as coordinator of the Master of Education Program in Teaching and Learning at Cabrini College, working with practicing teachers to improve student learning in the classroom. She is an associate professor in educational policy and leadership, teaching courses on diversity, multicultural education, and action research for teachers. Dr. Szpara completed training as a diversity educator at the University of Pennsylvania and regularly offers workshops for childhood educators through Pennsylvania Keys and the Better Kid Care Program at the Pennsylvania State University.

Candace M. Thompson is an assistant professor at University of North Carolina Wilmington having earned her PhD in social foundations of education. She teaches both graduate and undergraduate social foundations and multicultural education. She lives her research by engaging her students (and herself) in local schools and communities to support the development of cultural competence and commitments to social justice.

Jasmine Williams is a recent doctoral graduate in the Whitlowe R. Green College of Education at Prairie View A&M University. She earned her undergraduate degree in English from Spelman College and her MBA from Texas Woman's University. Her research interests include alternatives to traditional education for historically marginalized students, culturally responsive educational practices, and social justice-oriented leadership.

Made in United States
North Haven, CT
16 June 2023

37825088R00104